SPANISH
COOKING

**A WONDERFUL JOURNEY
THROUGH CULINARY DELIGHTS
IN SEARCH OF THE SECRETS
OF A SPLENDID COUNTRY**

BONECHI

HOW TO READ THE CHARTS

DIFFICULTY	FLAVOUR	NUTRITIONAL VALUE
● Easy	● Mild	● Low
●● Quite easy	●● Tasty	●● Medium
●●● Difficult	●●● Spicy	●●● High

Most of our recipes, especially those that require a certain amount of attention during their preparation, are illustrated with a series of step-by-step photographs to help the cook. We suggest you read the list of ingredients carefully (as well as the charts, which indicate how long it will take to prepare and cook the dishes, their difficulty, the strength of their flavour, their nutritional value), then every step of the method, all before attempting it. Then, of course — *bon appetit*!

A technical detail: where 'ground pimiento' is mentioned, whether in the list of ingredients or in the text of the method, this means the Spanish *pimentón*, a spice (not necessarily very hot) obtained from dried and ground *capsicum annuum*, fiery red in colour and strong in flavour. The type found in Spain is either *fuerte* (hot) or *dulce* (mild) and the choice depends upon personal taste and eating habit. This ground pimiento is an actual ingredient, necessary for the success of the recipe and not just an 'artistic touch' added to make the dishes more appetising. Some English speaking countries erroneously translate this ingredient with the word *paprika*, but this is not the Hungarian paprika, which is obtained from an Indian variety of small peppers with smaller pods and a more pungent fragrance; the *pimentón* spice is made from varieties that were brought over from the New World. Though paprika is different regards flavour, colour and gastronomic value, either its hot or mild strengths may be used instead of *pimentón*, or even the ground pimiento found in shops that sell biological produce.

ADDENDA

The recipe for *Faves al tombet* (page 105) and the two that follow (*Fabada Asturiana* and *Habas a la rondeña*) originally require the use of fresh broad beans, but they are equally delicious if made with other types of beans, especially the large, white Spanish butter beans. We have chosen this latter solution since the season for fresh butter beans is longer than that for broad beans; on the other hand, if dry butter beans are used, the dish can be made all year round. Nevertheless, when fresh broad beans are available, these must be used.

Project: Casa Editrice Bonechi
Series editor: Alberto Andreini
Concept and coordination: Paolo Piazzesi
Graphic design: Andrea Agnorelli and Maria Rosanna Malagrinò
Cover: Maria Rosanna Malagrinò
Make-up: Vanni Berti
Editing: Rina Bucci

Translation: Shona C. Dryburgh

Chef: Lisa Mugnai
Dietician: Dr. John Luke Hili

The photographs relative to the recipes are property of the Casa Editrice Bonechi photographic archives and were taken by Andrea Fantauzzo.

The other photographs used in this publication are property of the Casa Editrice Bonechi photographic archives and were taken by
Marco Bonechi, Luigi Di Giovine, Paolo Giambone, Andrea Pistolesi.
The photographs on pages 72 and 120 were taken by Maurizio Fraschetti.

© Copyright 2002
by CASA EDITRICE BONECHI, Firenze - Italia
E-mail: bonechi@bonechi.it   Internet: www.bonechi.it www.bonechi.com

Printed in Italy by Centro Stampa Editoriale Bonechi.

The cover, layout and artworks by the Casa Editrice Bonechi *graphic artists in this publication, are protected by international copyright.*

ISBN 88-476-0871-6

***

NOT ONLY PAELLA...

While award-ing deserved honours in this book to the famous and acclaimed Spanish cuisine, we have not forgotten to mention the most representative dishes of all the other regions. The basis of all good cooking is the use of good quality ingredients: olive oil is the prevalent cooking fat or dressing in the Mediterranean areas, whereas lard or suet is sometimes used in the central and northern areas. Naturally, fish is abundant on the table.

The use of rice and aubergines, saffron and almonds, peaches and apricots, brown sugar and honey in the recipes denotes the Jewish influence in the food. Spain also produces many types of cheese (*cabrales, mahón, manchego, roncal*, etc.) and excellent cured meats and salamis (*jamón serrano, butifarra, chorizo, morcilla*, etc.); these are all described underneath the recipes that require them. As for the enormous variety of wines – a separate book would be needed to describe them all. So, let's start our journey to explore the delights of Iberian cooking.

In the North, at the foot of the Pyrenees, the **Basque Counties** are famous throughout Europe for the way they cook fish and mountain fare. The particular dishes we have chosen for you can all be used to compile a typical Basque menu, from hors d'oeuvres to dessert: *gambas en gabardinas, atún encebollado, txangurro, marmitako, bacalao al pil-pil* or *bacalao a la vizcaína* (as eaten in Bilbao), *merluza a la kotxera* or *besugo a la donostiarra* (a typical San Sebastián dish), *huevos a la vasca, huevos a la vizcaína, piperrada* and *purrusalda* – and, to finish, a dessert of *intxaursalsa*. The dishes found in the green **Cantabrian** district of Santander, called 'La Montaña', are less famous

but are just as varied and delicious as those in the Basque areas, and even here the cooking is a marriage between the sea and the mountains: *mejillones a la marinera* and *jabalí a la montañesa*. Following the pilgrims' routes through the woodlands of **Asturias**, where there is no Moorish influence and where the main drink is *sidra* (cider) we come to Gijón and Oviedo: after a plate of the famous *fabada asturiana*, why not a taste of their *casadielles*? Then we reach wind-swept **Galicia**, the most western part of Spain that juts out into the Atlantic Ocean, the land of Saints and miracles, where the reflections of the mountains shimmer in the crystal-clear waters of the *rías*. Here the generous, unmistakably tasty fare of Vigo, La Coruña, Orense and Pontevedra is rightly famous and rivals Basque cuisine: a complete, typical menu can be prepared from *gambas en salsa gallega, pulpos a la gallega* or *vieiras a la gallega* (the famous *conchas peregrinas*, the 'Pilgrims' shells', or scallops in English, which remind us of the Path to Santiago), followed by *caldo gallego* (which has become a national dish), *empanada gallega, boguvante a la gallega, revuelto de gambas y grelos* (turnip broccoli), and ending up with *filloas dulces* or *leche frita*.

Inland, near the Basque region, lies **La Rioja**, which is famous for its wines and its *codornices en zurrón* and *patatas a la riojana*. Pamplona in woody **Navarra** is known all over for its trout fried in ham, and although the roots of the cuisine here are Basque, it is more similar to that found in **Aragona**, the historical region of mediaeval Spain, where we find Huesca, Teruel and Saragozza: here the *posadas*, the inns, are famous for their simple and hearty food like *chilindrón*, a special way of preparing lamb or chicken with tomatoes and sweet peppers, or like the dish we have selected for you, the delicious *coliflor al ajo arriero* (meaning, 'cauliflower as done by the mule-drivers').

We now reach the ancient heart of Christian Spain: **Castile and León**, the land of kings and warriors, crenellated castles and historical cities such as Ávila, Segovia, Valladolid, Burgos, León and Salamanca. The food here is rich and varied and the most popular dishes are *asados*, roasts, mainly of game: with the recipes from this area you can prepare a menu of hearty, genuine food for your table, like *arroz a la zamorana*, *hornazo castellano* (in a pastry crust), *liebre estofada a la castellana*, *ropa vieja* (a masterpiece of recycled leftovers), and *truchas a la zamorana*. The **Castile-La Mancha** area, which includes Toledo, Ciudad Real, Cuenca, Guadalajara and Albacete, is famous for its wines and cheeses; from the range of wholesome food here, very similar to that found in Lusitania, we have chosen *judías verdes a la castellana* and the sweet *torrijas*. While the hundreds of restaurants in cosmopolitan **Madrid** offer a wide range of international cooking, the traditional food is linked with Castile, León and La Mancha,

like the dishes we have chosen: *sopa al cuarto de hora*, *chuletas de cerdo*, the famous *cocido madrileño* (now a national dish), and *tortilla capuchina*.

In solitary **Estremadura**, with its pastures and woodlands bordering Portugal, and especially in cities like Badajoz and Alcántara, we can come across a genuine *sopa de ajo*, another dish acclaimed nation-wide, and *caldereta de cordero*.

Then we come to Barcelona, Gerona, Lérida, Tarragona and the Costa Brava – proud **Catalonia** bathed by the Mediterranean Sea, where the inhabitants closely guard their identity not only regards the language (noticeable in the names of many of the dishes) but also in their versatile but distinct cooking, where there is a tendency to blend sea flavours with those from the countryside (a vast range of dishes are called *mar i terra*), not to forget their excellent sauces like *romesco*, made of sweet peppers, and *sofrito*. Here there are influences from other regions in Spain (particularly from nearby Eastern regions, as can be seen in the *arros negre amb alli i oli*, in which the famous *allioli* sauce makes its appearance) as well as from Italy (mainly in the use of pasta, like in the *fideos a la catalana*) and from Provence. In Spanish cuisine, Catalan cooking vies for first place with that prepared in the Basque Counties, and together with the dishes mentioned above we can arrange a complete and very rich menu: *sopa de mejillones*, *asado de cerdo a la catalana*, *conejo al estilo tarraco-*

A view of Barcelona and the Sant Eulalia Cathedral.
On the previous page: a typical restaurant in the Barrio de Santa Cruz, Seville.

4

nense, pollo en samfaina (a sauce made of aubergines and sweet peppers), 'cap roig' with *salsa de ajo, rape en salsa de almendras, berenjenas a la catalana*, and ending up with the superb *crema catalana*. Down in the Eastern regions, where Valencia, Castellón de la Plana, Alicante and Murcia show more evident signs of Moorish influence, we come to the splendid coastline of Costa de Azahar and Costa Blanca where unforgettable dishes of fish, shellfish and seafood and are served in charming places like Elche, Benidorm and Javea. This is the homeland of rice dishes, introduced by the Moors, and of course, *paella*; with nearby Catalonia this area shares not only the language and traditions but also the colourful *zarzuela* and other delicacies for our menu, like *cigalas al ajo, arros amb crosta, jibias con setas, mejillones rellenos, tortilla murciana* and *faves* (beans) *al tombet*. The **Balearic Islands** of Majorca, Minorca, Ibiza and Formentera, which lie off the Catalonia coast, have similar linguistic and culinary traditions though enriched by French and Italian influences. Besides the excellent fish that definitely bears the crown in these islands, our list includes *greixera de macarrones, sopa de col mallorquina, tumbet de pescado* (a mixed fish casserole with aubergines and potatoes), *huevos mallorquinos* with the typi-

cal *sobresata, berenjenas rellenas* and, as a dessert, *ensuimadas mallorquinas*, made with lard, and *flaō*.

The Arabian influence becomes evident in beautiful **Andalusia** where, among orchards and olive groves, the superb Jerez de la Frontera wines (English Sherry) are produced; these are rivalled by the famous Malaga sweet wines. Here we have come to Granada, towered over by the peaks of the Sierra Nevada, magical Seville, cultured Córdoba, Cadice, the port to the New World and famous for its fishing fleets, Almería, Huelva, Ronda and Jaén. Thanks to the riches offered by both the sea and the land, Andalusian food deserves a top rank place in Spanish cooking; from the enormous range of dishes we have chosen *brochetas de Almería, pinchitos* or *tortillitas de camarones a la gaditana*, the famous *gazpacho* (not to be confused with *gazpachuelo*), which has become a national dish along with *huevos a la flamen-*

The unmistakable Punta Roja, near El Médano in southern Tenerife (Canary Islands), and a couple of dancers in Ibiza (Balearic Islands) in the typical costume of the island.

5

A view of the splendid Generalife Gardens, in the Granada Alhambra.

ca; then *pato a la sevillana*, made with local, juicy olives, *pollo al Jerez, estofado a la andaluza, pez espada a la malagueña, habas a la rondeña* and, to finish, a dessert of *brazo de gitano*.

On the last part of our culinary journey we reach the **Canary Islands**, the volcanic archipelago in the middle of the Atlantic Ocean, where the climate is mild; dominated by the peak of Mount Teide on the island of Tenerife, these islands offer exotic food which has very little in common with the traditions of the mainland, the main influence here being African. With the recipes from this area you can prepare, besides *gofio*, the delicious sauces called *mojos* (*papas con mojos*), *puchero canario*, reminiscent of Creole flavours, *conejo al hinojo, cabrito al salmorejo, pollo embarrado, encebollado de pescado, pulpos canarios, sancocho canario*, accompanied by the typical and unusual *papas arrugadas*. And to finish, *buñuelos de boniatos*, which are sweet potatoes, and *tortitas de plátanos*, made with the exquisite bananas the Islands are famous for.

A FEW WORDS FROM THE DIETICIAN

*S*panish cuisine comes under what is called the 'Mediterranean Diet'; a traditional habit of healthy eating that is envied all over the world. On the whole, this diet helps prevent arteriosclerotic degeneration and cardiovascular diseases such as ictus and myocardiac infarction.

The main characteristics of the Mediterranean diet are: a prevalence of calories derived from carbohydrates, particularly the complex forms; next come starches from cereals such as wheat and rice; a high content of vegetable fibres, especially the insoluble kind found in green leaf vegetables, but also the soluble fibres contained in fruit; the fat used in cooking and for dressings is almost exclusively extra virgin olive oil, which provides the 'good' oleic acid (excellent if taken in moderation); moderate use of animal proteins that provide 'good' fats, such as the polyunsaturated fats found in white meat and fish, particularly in 'blue' fish (the inexpensive type caught in local waters).

No matter how the food is presented, whether as an all-in-one dish, as a separate delicacy, or with pasta or rice – the fundamental characteristics are all the same: all the populations in the Mediterranean basin tend to take advantage of the biological nutrients provided by Nature, and as a result they follow what we call the 'Mediterranean Diet'. In Spanish cuisine, this feature is further enhanced due to the strong Arabian influence throughout history.

TABLE OF CONTENTS

The Real Plaza de la Maestranza, in Seville, the beautiful and world-famous bullring.

TAPAS AND ENTREMESES

Tapas *are the colourful snacks and appetisers found in abundance on the counters of particular cafés and snack-bars and propose a different, light-hearted supper, and the entremeses are hors d'œuvres of seafood or country fare: the choice is vast, mainly seafood and shellfish, in which flavour is enhanced even further by means of delicate or spicy sauces, though the wide range of Spain's superb cheeses plays an important role as well.*

1

BROCHETAS DE ALMERÍA

Mixed marinated skewers ✒ *Andalusia*

Lean pork, chicken or beef
  (in one, firm piece),
  500 g (1 lb 2 oz)
Smoked bacon, 180g (8 oz)
2-3 spring onions
2 firm salad tomatoes
One yellow bell pepper
3-4 slices of farmhouse bread
  without crusts, cubed

For the marinade:
Pine nuts (a small handful)
Ground cinnamon, nutmeg
  and saffron
Parsley (one sprig)
Dry white wine
Salt and freshly ground pepper
Olive oil

Serves: 8	
Preparation: 20'+3-4h	
Cooking: 7-10'	
Difficulty: ●	
Flavour: ●●	
Kcal (per serving): 709	
Proteins (per serving): 20	
Fats (per serving): 50	
Nutritional value: ●●●	

1 Pound the pine nuts to a paste-like consistency in a mortar, add half a teaspoon of cinnamon, a pinch of grated nutmeg and a sachet of saffron. Rub this paste delicately all over the meat and place in a bowl to marinade, together with the chopped parsley, one glass of white wine and 4-5 tablespoons of oil. Turn the meat over every now and then. In the meantime, wash and prepare the vegetables: cut the spring onions into regular-sized pieces, and the tomatoes and the pepper (having removed the seeds and fibrous parts) into small triangles.

2 After 3-4 hours, drain the meat (keep the marinade liquid) and cube. Trim the rind off the bacon before cutting it. Using long skewers, pierce the meat and bacon pieces alternately with bits of onion, triangles of tomato and pepper, cubes of bread. Sprinkle with salt and place on a hot grill for 6-7 minutes, turning over every minute until all sides have browned, and basting with the marinade liquid. As an alternative, place the skewers in a large ovenproof dish, brush with some of the marinade liquid, and cook in a hot oven (220°C; 410°F)) for 10 minutes. Baste again whenever necessary. Serve piping hot sprinkled with freshly ground pepper.

CIGALAS AL AJO

Garlic scampi ☞ *Eastern regions and Andalusia*

1 Prepare the scampi taking care to eliminate the shell and dorsal vein (intestine), rinse and dry. Rinse and prepare the pimientos by removing the stalks and seeds, dry and chop into tiny pieces (if dried pimientos are used, just remove the seeds). Peel the garlic cloves and slice each lengthwise into four.

2 Toss the scampi, pimientos and garlic in a frying pan with 5-6 tablespoons of oil for 3 minutes, adding salt and pepper to taste. Serve immediately.

Scampi, 1 Kg (2 1/4 lb)
4-5 small, fresh pimientos
One head of garlic
Salt and pepper
Olive oil

Serves:	8
Preparation:	15'
Cooking:	3'
Difficulty:	●
Flavour:	● ● ●
Kcal (per serving):	237
Proteins (per serving):	20
Fats (per serving):	16
Nutritional value:	● ● ●

GAMBAS EN GABARDINA

Batter-fried king prawns ☞ *Basque Counties*

King prawns, 1 Kg (2 ¼ lb)
2 lemons and green lettuce
   (for garnish)
Frying oil

For the batter:
Plain flour, 180 g
   (6 oz; 1 ½ cups)
2 egg whites
Salt, Cayenne pepper
Olive oil

Serves:	8
Preparation:	15'+10'
Cooking:	10'
Difficulty:	●●
Flavour:	●●
Kcal (per serving):	620
Proteins (per serving):	38
Fats (per serving):	39
Nutritional value:	●●●

1 Prepare the batter by blending the flour with a pinch of salt, 3-4 tablespoons of oil, a pinch of Cayenne pepper and sufficient tepid water (about 3 dl; 12 fl. oz) to obtain a batter with a smooth, dropping consistency . Place the batter to one side to 'stand'. Rinse the prawns, open them and remove the dorsal veins. Beat the egg whites until stiff and blend gently into the batter mixture.

2 Put the prawns into the batter and leave for about 10 minutes (until completely and thickly covered). Gently drop them into very hot oil and fry quickly until crisp. Remove as soon as ready with a draining spoon and leave to dry on kitchen paper. Serve as a starter on a bed of lettuce and surrounded by lemon slices.

GAMBAS EN SALSA GALLEGA

Prawns in spicy sauce ☞ *Galicia*

Shrimp and prawn tails, 500 g
  (1 lb 2 oz)
3-4 cloves of garlic
Ground pimiento
One dried red pimiento
Salt, white peppercorns
Red wine vinegar
Olive oil

Serves:	6
Preparation:	15'
Cooking:	5'
Difficulty:	●
Flavour:	● ● ●
Kcal (per serving):	170
Proteins (per serving):	6
Fats (per serving):	15
Nutritional value:	● ● ●

Blanch the shrimp and prawn tails in slightly salted, boiling water for 5 minutes; drain well and place on the serving dish. Peel the garlic cloves, pound to a paste in a mortar, then add a teaspoonful of ground pimiento, the dried pimiento (seeded and chopped finely), a pinch of salt, 2-3 tablespoons of vinegar and sufficient oil (approx. one wine-glass) to obtain a sauce into which each guest will dip the cooked seafood. Sprinkle freshly ground pepper over the sauce at the last minute and serve this simple but delicious starter with dry white wine at cellar temperature.

MEJILLONES A LA MARINERA

Fisherman-style mussels ☞ *Cantabria*

Mussels,
  approx. 1 Kg (2 1/4 lb)
Farmhouse bread, 3-4 slices
3-4 garlic cloves
One fresh red pimiento
Dry breadcrumbs, 30 g (3 tbsp)
Parsley, one sprig
Dry white wine
Olive oil

Serves:	6-8
Preparation:	15'
Cooking:	6-7'
Difficulty:	●
Flavour:	● ●
Kcal (per serving):	376
Proteins (per serving):	12
Fats (per serving):	17
Nutritional value:	● ● ●

Toast the bread slices in the oven, or under the grill. Cut into finger-size strips. Using a stiff brush, clean the mussels, remove the 'whiskers' which emerge from the valves, and rinse well without drying them; put them into a large pan together with the finely chopped garlic, a drizzle of oil and a drinking glass of water and wine in equal proportions. Bring to the boil, put the lid on the pan and allow the mussels to open. Sprinkle the mussels with the breadcrumbs mixed with chopped parsley and pimiento (without seeds) and leave to flavour for one or two minutes on a low flame. Remove the mussels, remove the empty shell from every one and arrange the full ones on a serving dish with the strips of toasted bread around them. Pour the filtered cooking liquid into a small bowl to accompany the mussels.

PAPAS CON MOJOS

Potatoes with green and red sauces 🖝 *Canary Islands*

10-12 new potatoes
  (not too small)

For the red sauce:
2-3 cloves of garlic
One fresh red pimiento
Caraway seeds
Fresh oregano
Vinegar
Salt and pepper
Olive oil

For the green sauce:
4 cloves of garlic
One fresh red pimiento
Parsley (a good sized bunch)
Coriander seeds
Caraway seeds
Fresh oregano
Vinegar
Salt and pepper
Olive oil

Serves:	6-8
Preparation:	20'
Cooking:	10'
Difficulty:	●
Flavour:	● ●
Kcal (per serving):	274
Proteins (per serving):	1
Fats (per serving):	25
Nutritional value:	● ●

Wash the potatoes, boil until cooked (but still very firm) in slightly salted water, gently remove skins and cut into even sized disks. Each guest will dip a disk at a time into one of the sauces.

1 Pound in a mortar (or in a food mixer) the skinned garlic and the pimiento; using a small bowl, mix the pounded paste with a teaspoonful of ground pimiento, half a teaspoon of caraway seeds, the leaves of a sprig of oregano, 3-4 tablespoons of oil, 3 tablespoons of vinegar and sufficient water to obtain a fluid but thick sauce, which will then be put into a bowl or sauce-boat.

2 Pound in a mortar (or in a food mixer) the peeled garlic cloves, the pimiento and a teaspoon of coriander seeds, and place in a bowl; add the finely chopped parsley, a small pinch (or tip of teaspoon) of caraway seeds, the leaves from a sprig of oregano, 3 tablespoons of oil, 3 of vinegar and sufficient water to make a soft consistency sauce, which will then be placed in a bowl next to the other one.

15

PULPOS A LA GALLEGA

Octopus with potatoes ☞ *Galicia*

One medium-small
 (or several tiny) octopus,
 5-600 g (1 ¼ lb)
2-3 potatoes
Ground pimiento
Coarse salt
Olive oil

Serves:	4-6
Preparation:	15′
Cooking:	40′+20′
Difficulty:	● ●
Flavour:	● ●
Kcal (per serving):	294
Proteins (per serving):	14
Fats (per serving):	16
Nutritional value:	● ● ●

Prepare the octopus (or the tiny ones) by turning the sac inside out to remove the interiors, eliminating the 'tooth' and eyes; rinse it well and place in a pan full of cold and slightly salted water. Cover with the lid and bring to the boil; lower the heat to minimum and leave to simmer for 30-40 minutes (the time depends upon whether a single octopus or several small ones are being used). Turn off the heat and allow the octopus to cool in the cooking water. In the meantime, boil the potatoes (do not over boil; they must remain firm), peel them while still warm and cut into cubes.

Remove the octopus when cold, drain well and cut into small, regular sized pieces; mix these together with the potatoes in a dish.

Flavour to taste with a pinch of coarse salt, a teaspoon of ground pimiento and sufficient olive oil.

Serve at room temperature on a wooden board.

QUESO FRITO

Fried cheese titbits ☛ *La Mancha*

C ut the cheese into slices one centimetre ($^1/_3$ inch) thick, remove the crust and cut the slices into even triangles (or strips). Dip into the flour (shaking off any excess flour) then into the beaten eggs (where they must be left for a few minutes); remove from the beaten eggs and dip into the breadcrumbs until evenly coated.
Deep fry quickly until golden (the cheese should not be allowed to melt), dry on kitchen paper and serve hot.

Queso manchego
  (medium mature),
  500 g (1 lb 2 oz)
2 eggs
Plain flour, 40 g (4 tbsp)
Dry breadcrumbs, 50 g (5 tbsp)
Frying oil

Serves: 6-8	
Preparation: 15'	
Cooking: 10'	
Difficulty: ●	
Flavour: ●	
Kcal (per serving): 589	
Proteins (per serving): 21	
Fats (per serving): 48	
Nutritional value: ● ● ●	

TORTILLITAS DE CAMARONES A LA GADITANA

Shrimp fritters ☞ *Andalusia*

1 Peel the onion and chop it finely with the pimiento (without seeds). Put into a bowl and add the chopped parsley together with the rinsed and dried shrimps broken into pieces. Mix well.

2 To the mixture above, add the flour, half a glass of wine, the yeast and sufficient cold water (just under 4 dl; 16 fl oz) to make a fairly stiff batter, using a whisk or hand-mixer. Leave to stand for 2-3 hours in a cool place.

3 Taking a tablespoon of batter at a time, drop the *tortillitas* into very hot oil; turn them over with a draining spoon so that both sides become golden crisp.

4 As soon as they are ready, remove one at a time and drain on a serving dish covered with kitchen paper; sprinkle with small quantities of salt and serve hot.

The imposing and unique Mezquita-Catedral in Cordoba, Andalusia: built by Arabs in 786, the mosque was transformed for Roman Catholic worship in the XIII century, after the 'Reconquista', and became a cathedral in 1523.

Shrimp tails, shelled,
   200 g (6 oz)
1 medium-sized onion
Plain flour, 250 g (2 cups)
Baker's yeast, fresh,
   15 g (1 tbsp)
1 red pimiento
Dry white wine

Parsley
Salt
Frying oil

Serves: 4
Preparation: 15'+3h
Cooking: 15'
Difficulty: ● ●
Flavour: ● ●
Kcal (per serving): 557
Proteins (per serving): 14
Fats (per serving): 26
Nutritional value: ● ● ●

VIEIRAS A LA GALLEGA

Oven-baked scallops ☞ *Galicia*

12 scallops
1 onion
1 clove of garlic
Ground pimiento
Dry breadcrumbs,
   25 g (2 1/2 tbsp)
2 lemons
Parsley
Brandy
Dry white wine
Salt and pepper
Olive oil

Serves:	6
Preparation:	15'
Cooking:	6-7'
Difficulty:	●
Flavour:	● ●
Kcal (per serving):	373
Proteins (per serving):	6
Fats (per serving):	16
Nutritional value:	● ● ●

1 No heating is required to open the scallops: simply force the blade of a knife between the two valves of the shell and prise open. Rinse the molluscs well, extract them, remove the stomach (black) and the fringes (brown), and separate the white (the 'nut') from the 'coral'. Save the deeper halves of the shells, and put the 'nuts' back in these and arrange in an ovenproof dish.

2 Gently fry (until transparent) the chopped onion and garlic in a pan with 3-4 tablespoons of oil; add the 'corals' finely chopped together with a teaspoonful of ground pimiento. Mix well to allow the flavours to combine. Add half a glass of wine, then a small liqueur glass of brandy. Salt to taste. Allow the sauce to reduce (about 2 min) then pour it over the 'nuts' in the shells. Chop a sprig of parsley and mix with the breadcrumbs; sprinkle the mixture over the scallops, add a drizzle of oil to each and place under the grill of the oven until golden brown on the surface. Serve immediately with lemon wedges.

SOUPS, PASTA AND RICE DISHES

Simplicity and imagination, the two mainstays of Spanish cooking, together in an outstanding variety of delicious dishes: from warm caldo gallego, hearty and of northern influence, to cool gazpacho, nutritious and ideal in the heat of Summer, without neglecting the pasta dishes that make Italian housewives green with envy!

2

ARROS AMB CROSTA

Oven-browned rice ☛ *Eastern regions*

Rice for timbales,
  500 g (¹/₂ lb; 2 ³/₄ cups)
6 eggs
Butifarra (see below),
  120 g (4 ¹/₂ oz)
Leftover cooked white or red
  meat, 150 g (6 oz)
Lean pork, 100 g (4 oz)
2 ripe tomatoes
Cooked chickpeas, 100 g (4 oz)
Chicken or vegetable broth
  (made with bouillon cubes),
  1.5 litres (2 ¹/₂ pt)
Saffron
Salt and pepper
Olive oil

Serves:	6
Preparation:	15'
Cooking:	40'
Difficulty:	● ●
Flavour:	● ●
Kcal (per serving):	739
Proteins (per serving):	31
Fats (per serving):	33
Nutritional value:	● ● ●

Butifarra is a cured sausage typical of the Catalonia and Eastern regions, but is found all over Spain. Butifarra blanca is a fat, juicy but firm sausage (like a Scottish white pudding) made of minced pork (loin fillet and belly) and – sometimes – onion, garlic, cinnamon, cloves and wine, and can be pan-cooked or grilled (it can be substituted with other types of spiced sausage, as long as they are not hot in flavour). Butifarra negra, which is not so common, contains pig blood (rather like a 'black pudding') and chopped mint.

1 Slice the *butifarra* into rounds and gently fry them in an earthenware casserole (ovenproof) with 5-6 tablespoons of oil, turning them over so that they brown on both sides. Remove with a draining spoon and keep in a warm place. Remove the seeds from the tomatoes, chop the pulp and gently fry for five minutes in the oil left in the casserole, together with the diced lean pork. Add the rice and the hot broth; flavour with salt and pepper to taste, adding a sachet of saffron. Mix well.

2 Bring to the boil then lower the heat to minimum; add the browned *butifarra*, the left over meat and the chickpeas. Simmer, mixing every now and then, until the rice is just cooked (*al dente*) but not soft; this will take approx. 15 minutes. Remove the pan from the heat, smooth the surface of the rice and cover it with the eggs beaten with a pinch of salt. Place in a heated oven (200°C; 375°F) until the egg mixture is cooked and the surface is golden brown.

ARROZ A LA ZAMORANA

Rice with meat and vegetables

☛ Castile and León

Rice for soups, 300 g
  (10 oz; 1 2/3 cups)
1 pig's trotter and a piece of pig
  cheek (or ear)
Cured raw ham (prosciutto),
  100 g (4 oz)
Unsmoked bacon, 100 g (4 oz)
1 onion
4 cloves of garlic
2 small turnips
Bouquet garni (bay leaf,
  oregano, parsley and thyme),
  tied
Salt and pepper
Lard, 40 g (1 1/2 oz)

Serves: 4-6	
Preparation: 20'	
Cooking: 2h 20'	
Difficulty: ● ●	
Flavour: ● ●	
Kcal (per serving): 603	
Proteins (per serving): 18	
Fats (per serving): 35	
Nutritional value: ● ● ●	

1 Hold the trotter over a flame to eliminate any bristles, wash it well, divide it into two lengthwise (without separating the two parts) and place it in a casserole with the cheek (cleaned and trimmed), the bouquet garni, salt and pepper, then pour in a litre and a half (2 1/2 pt) of cold water. Cover the pan and bring slowly to the boil; simmer for a couple of hours. When cooked, remove the trotter (save the broth, filter it and keep it warm), bone it and cut the meat (including the fat and cartilage) into small pieces. Peel the turnips and onions. Chop the onion with the garlic and gently fry in an ovenproof earthenware casserole with the previously melted lard (about the size of a walnut); add the finely diced turnip and ham.

2 After two minutes, add the pieces of trotter meat and the rice; increase the heat under the pan to allow the flavours to combine then add the filtered broth, and salt and pepper to taste. Lower the heat to medium and cook for about ten minutes. Remove the pan from the heat and eliminate the bouquet garni; sprinkle the rice with the bacon cut into strips and brown under the grill for 4-5 minutes.

ARROS NEGRE AMB ALL I OLI

Black rice with garlic and oil sauce ☞ *Catalonia*

1 Scrub the shells of the mussels and remove the 'whiskers', rinse and put into a pan with a lid, adding enough water to just cover the mussels; place the covered pan on a high heat to open the valves. As soon as they are open, switch off the heat and re-

move the mussels from their liquid, extract the pulp and discard the shells.

2 Prepare the squids (or cuttlefish), eliminate the interiors (saving 4-5 ink sacs), and rinse them well; if they are very small, leave them whole, otherwise cut them into pieces by separating the sacs from the tentacles. Clean the vegetables and prepare them for use: gently fry the chopped onion with the finely diced pepper in a casserole (preferably earthenware) in 5-6 tablespoons of oil. Add the squids and cook on medium heat for 3-4 minutes.

3 Add the washed tomatoes. After 4-5 minutes, add the filtered liquid in which the mussels have opened, lower the heat to minimum and allow the liquid to reduce for about 20 minutes. Add the rice and approx. half a litre (3/4 pt) of hot water; add salt to taste, then the pimiento left whole. While the rice simmers, stir every now and then and add more hot water whenever necessary.

The famous and unusual Casa Milà, better known as 'La Pedrera': designed by the outstanding artist, Antoni Gaudí, this work of art stands on the Passeig de Gracia in Barcelona.

Rice for risotto, 250 g (8 oz; 1 1/3 cups)	Cherry tomatoes, 150 g (5 oz)	Serves: 4
Tiny squids or cuttlefish, approx. 500 g (1 lb 2 oz)	3 cloves of garlic	**Preparation:** 25'
Mussels, 500 g (1 lb 2 oz)	1 fresh red pimiento	**Cooking:** 1h ca.
Shrimp tails, 100 g (4 oz)	Dry white wine	**Difficulty:** ● ● ●
1 onion	Salt	**Flavour:** ● ●
1 green sweet pepper	Olive oil	**Kcal (per serving):** 538
		Proteins (per serving): 31
		Fats (per serving): 14
		Nutritional value: ● ●

4 While this is cooking, prepare the sauce: pound the peeled garlic cloves in a mortar with a pinch of salt; transfer to a bowl and add a glass of oil, mixing well. Dilute the ink from the sacs in half a glass of wine then add this to the rice when 15 minutes of the cooking time have passed. Simmer for about another five minutes, or until the rice is cooked but still firm (*al dente*); remove from the heat. At this point, add the shelled mussels and the shrimp tails, and delicately blend in a tablespoon of the garlic sauce. The remaining sauce will be served in a bowl next to the rice dish.

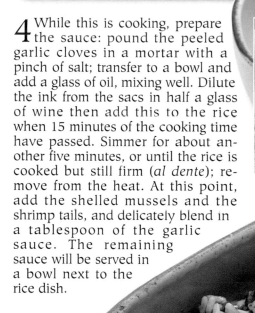

4

SOPA AL CUARTO DE HORA

'Fifteen-minute' rice soup ☛ *Madrid*

Rice, 150 g (5 oz; 1 1/4 cups)
Clams, 1 Kg (2 1/4 lb)
Scampi, 600 g (1 1/4 lb)
Cured raw ham (prosciutto)
 in one slice, 100 g (4 oz)
Shelled peas, 100 g (4 oz)
2 eggs
1 onion
1 tomato
Saffron
Parsley
Salt and pepper
Olive oil

Serves: 4-6

Preparation: 25'

Cooking: 15'+15'

Difficulty: ● ●

Flavour: ● ●

Kcal (per serving): 589

Proteins (per serving): 40

Fats (per serving): 31

Nutritional value: ● ● ●

1 Put the clams in a pan with enough water to just cover them, cover with a lid and allow them to open very slowly over a low heat. Shell about 2/3 of them (the other third will serve as garnish), keep them in a warm place and filter the remaining liquid. Gently boil the scampi in slightly salted water for about 5-6 minutes; remove them from the pan, remove their shells and dorsal veins. Save this cooking liquid as well, filter it and add it to the clam liquid. Boil the eggs for 7 minutes and shell them.

2 Skin and chop the onion and stew it gently in a pan (preferably earthenware) until transparent with 5-6 tablespoons of olive oil; skin the tomatoes, remove the seeds and dice them before adding them, together with the diced ham, to the pan. Let the flavours combine for a few minutes then add the rice, the scampi, the peas; dilute a sachet of saffron in the previously filtered clam and scampi liquid (adding sufficient hot water to obtain 1.5 litres (2 1/2 pt) and pour over the other ingredients. Bring to the boil then lower the heat to minimum; add the shelled clams and the scampi. Flavour with salt and pepper to taste and allow to simmer for about 5 minutes. Serve the *sopa* sprinkled with the finely chopped boiled eggs and parsley and garnished with the remaining clams in their shells.

CALDO GALLEGO

Bean, vegetable and meat soup ☛ *Galicia*

1 About 4-5 hours before starting, put the beans in a pan and cover completely with cold water. Put the spare-ribs in a bowl and cover with warm water; leave them in the water for the same length of time as the beans (fresh spare-ribs can be used instead of the salt-cured type and do not require steeping). Drain both the beans and the spare-ribs and put them into a casserole (preferably earthenware); add the cubed lean pork and cover with cold water. Place the pan on the stove and bring to the boil; remove the scum from the top of the broth. Add the lard, cover with a lid and lower the heat to minimum; simmer for one hour or longer.

2 While the broth is cooking, clean the broccoli and break into small pieces, peel and dice the potatoes, skin the garlic and add all these ingredients to the broth together with a teaspoon of ground pimiento. Put the lid back on the casserole and simmer slowly for a further 30 minutes or longer; remove the lid for the last ten minutes of this cooking time in order to thicken the liquid (if an even thicker consistency is preferred, remove a ladle of potatoes and beans, cream them in a food mixer and return to the casserole). Serve the soup hot but not boiling; the spare-ribs can be boned before serving if desired.

Dry Spanish white beans
(butter beans),
250 g (8 oz; 1 ¹/₄ cups)
Salt-cured pork spare-ribs,
300 g (12 oz)
Lean pork, 200 g (8 oz)
Turnip broccoli, 250 g (10 oz)
2-3 potatoes
1 clove of garlic
Ground pimiento
Salt and pepper
Lard, 40 g (2 oz; 3-4 tbsp)

Serves: 4	
Preparation: 20'+4-5h	
Cooking: 1h 30'	
Difficulty: ●●	
Flavour: ●●	
Kcal (per serving): 553	
Proteins (per serving): 39	
Fats (per serving): 18	
Nutritional value: ●●●	

FIDEOS A LA CATALANA

Spicy spaghetti with cured meats ☛ *Catalonia*

Fideos (thin or ribbon spaghetti),
  350 g (14 oz)
Pork spare-ribs, 200 g (8 oz)
1 pimiento sausage
Butifarra (see page 22) ,
  100 g (4 oz)
1 onion
2 ripe tomatoes
Ground pimiento and cinnamon
Parsley
Shelled and blanched hazelnuts,
  almonds and pine-nuts
  (1 tbsp of each)
Chicken broth (ready made),
  1.5 litres (2 1/2 pt)
Saffron
Dry breadcrumbs
Mature cheese for grating
  (optional)
Lard, 30 g (1 oz; 3 tbsp)

Serves: 4	
Preparation: 20'	
Cooking: 30'	
Difficulty: ● ●	
Flavour: ● ●	
Kcal (per serving): 762	
Proteins (per serving): 33	
Fats (per serving): 36	
Nutritional value: ● ● ●	

Cut the spare-ribs into tiny pieces and brown them in the melted lard in a casserole (preferably earthenware); when nicely browned, add the chopped onion and allow to stew slowly. Add the chopped tomatoes (without seeds) and a pinch of ground pimiento; allow the flavours to blend for about 4-5 minutes. Skin the sausage and crumble the meat into the casserole along with the *butifarra* cut into disks and the broth; bring to the boil and add the pasta. Lower the heat to minimum. Ground in a mortar (or in a food mixer) the hazelnuts, almonds, pine nuts and garlic, adding a sachet of saffron, a pinch of cinnamon, a sprig of parsley and 2 tablespoons of breadcrumbs; dilute the paste obtained with a little broth and add this mixture to the soup simmering in the casserole. Remove from the heat when the pasta is almost cooked (*al dente*) and serve; flakes of mature cheese may be sprinkled over the soup before serving.

GAZPACHO

Cold vegetable soup ☞ *Andalusia*

1 Wash all the vegetables well; peel the cucumber and cut it into tiny pieces; skin the tomatoes and cut into tiny cubes; slice the onions into thin rings; prepare the pepper by removing the seeds and fibrous parts and chop. Put all these ingredients into a bowl; add the crushed cloves of garlic and the finely crumbled slice of crustless bread. Add a tablespoon of red vinegar, one of olive oil, and a pinch of salt. Mix well.

2 Transfer the mixture obtained to a food mixer (according to the quantity being prepared, this step may have to be repeated several times) to obtain a smooth and creamy consistency; taste for salt, adjusting if necessary, and place in the fridge, where it must remain for a couple of hours before serving time. Garnish the *gazpacho* at will and serve accompanied by slices or strips of toasted bread. If a hotter flavour is desired, add a pinch of ground pimiento to the vegetables in the food mixer.

6 ripe tomatoes
1 cucumber
1 sweet pepper
2 spring onions
2-3 cloves of garlic
4-6 slices of farmhouse bread +
   1 slice without crust
Red wine vinegar
Salt
Olive oil

Serves:	4
Preparation:	20'+2h
Difficulty:	●
Flavour:	●●
Kcal (per serving):	327
Proteins (per serving):	8
Fats (per serving):	4
Nutritional value:	●

Mayonnaise, the pride of French cuisine, is believed by some experts on the matter to have originated in Spain. To make the quantity required for this recipe, put two egg yolks into a small bowl with a pinch of salt. Pour a drop of olive oil over the yolks (about 2 wine-glasses will be needed in the end) and start stirring gently with a wooden spoon, with an even rhythm and always in the same direction (or use the special part of your food mixer). When the mixture starts to become dense, pour in the rest of the olive oil very gradually and with a steady hand (do not stop stirring); as a final touch, add the juice of a squeezed lemon (or 2-3 teaspoons of white wine vinegar).

GAZPACHUELO

Turbot and mayonnaise soup ☞ *Andalusia*

Turbot, approx. 600 g (1 ¼ lb)
Potatoes, 500 g (1 lb 2 oz)
Mayonnaise (see above), 300 g (12 oz; 1 ¼ cups)
1 stalk of celery
1 bay leaf
Sprig of parsley
Red wine vinegar
Salt

Serves:	4
Preparation:	25'
Cooking:	35'
Difficulty:	● ●
Flavour:	● ●
Kcal (per serving):	798
Proteins (per serving):	28
Fats (per serving):	62
Nutritional value:	● ● ●

Gut, skin and fillet the turbot. Save the head, tail, fins and bones and put them into a casserole with approximately one litre (1 ⅔ pt) of cold water, the cleaned celery cut into pieces, the sprig of parsley, bay leaf and a pinch of salt. Bring to the boil, cover, turn down the heat to minimum and simmer gently for 15 minutes. In the meantime, peal the potatoes, rinse and dry them and cut into cubes. Pass the fish broth through a fine sieve (no solid parts must pass through) into a casserole. Add the potatoes and slowly bring the broth to a boil again; simmer for about 15 minutes then gently add the turbot fillets cut into rectangular pieces. Simmer for a further five minutes, tasting for salt. Remove the fish and the potatoes with a draining spoon and put into a soup tureen. Allow the broth to cool slightly, then pour it into a bowl; blend in the prepared mayonnaise very delicately and pour the mixture obtained over the fish and potatoes in the tureen. Add two tablespoons of white wine vinegar, stir and serve.

GREIXERA DE MACARRONES

Macaroni pie ☛ *Balearic Islands*

1 Boil the eggs for 7 minutes then remove them from the water; allow them to cool before shelling them. Bring to the boil approx. 2.5 litres (3 ¾ pt) of slightly salted water and toss the rigatoni in it; cook until ¾ of the time indicated on the packet. Drain and put into a frying pan along with the milk; slowly bring to the boil, lower the heat to minimum and finishing cooking the rigatoni, stirring frequently.

2 At the last moment, add grated cheese to taste and a pinch of ground cinnamon; taste for salt and mix again. Transfer the rigatoni to a buttered ovenproof dish, cover with slices of boiled egg and sprinkle with more ground cinnamon. Place under the grill until golden brown on top (4-5 min) and serve immediately.

Rigatoni pasta, 350 g (14 oz)
4 eggs
Milk, 2.5 dl (10 fl oz)
Mature *Mahón* cheese
   (or *manchego*, or even
   Parmesan)
Ground cinnamon
Salt
Butter, 80 g (3 oz; 3 tbsp)

Serves:	4
Preparation:	15′
Cooking:	35′
Difficulty:	● ●
Flavour:	● ●
Kcal (per serving):	626
Proteins (per serving):	25
Fats (per serving):	34
Nutritional value:	● ● ●

SOPA DE AJO

Garlic soup ☛ *Estremadura*

5-6 slices of stale farmhouse
  bread
1 head of garlic
Ground pimiento
Chicken broth, 1.5 litres
  (2 1/2 pt)
4 egg yolks or grated cheese
  (both optional)
Salt and pepper
Olive oil

Serves:	4
Preparation:	20'
Cooking:	35'
Difficulty:	● ●
Flavour:	● ● ●
Kcal (per serving):	507
Proteins (per serving):	20
Fats (per serving):	26
Nutritional value:	● ●

Gently fry the diced bread in a casserole with 4-5 tablespoons of oil; after about 2-3 minutes, add the chopped cloves of the head of garlic, a teaspoon of ground pimiento, the broth, salt and pepper. Cover the casserole and simmer for about 20 minutes. In the meantime, turn on the oven, setting it at 200°C (375°F). Divide the *sopa* into four individual ovenproof ramekins and place them in the heated oven for about ten minutes. Serve immediately. If desired, a generous amount of grated cheese, or one egg yolk in each ramekin, may be added before putting them into the oven.

SOPA DE COL MALLORQUINA

Cabbage soup ☛ *Balearic Islands*

1 white cabbage
4-5 slices wholemeal bread, 400 g (1 lb)
2 onions
2 ripe tomatoes
3-4 cloves of garlic
2 fresh small green pimientos
Vegetable broth (using bouillon cubes), approx. 1 litre (1 1/2 pt)
Ground pimiento
Parsley
Salt and pepper
Olive oil

Serves:	4-6
Preparation:	20'
Cooking:	25'
Difficulty:	● ● ●
Flavour:	● ●
Kcal (per serving)	456
Proteins (per serving):	13
Fats (per serving):	14
Nutritional value:	● ●

1 Wash and prepare all the vegetables for use. Slice the bread into strips the width of a finger; gently fry these in an earthenware casserole with 7-8 tablespoons of oil. Drain and put to one side. Slowly stew the chopped onions in the same oil; after about 3-4 minutes, add the chopped garlic, the diced tomatoes and peppers, and the finely sliced cabbage. Increase the heat under the casserole and stir-fry the vegetables for about 3-4 minutes.

2 Add the chopped sprig of parsley, a teaspoon of ground pimiento, salt and pepper. Pour in the broth and bring to the boil; lower the heat, cover the casserole and simmer for about 10 minutes. Add the fried bread and simmer for another 7-8 minutes. Cool the soup to a certain degree before serving sprinkled with chopped parsley. This dish is excellent even the day after.

PUCHERO CANARIO

Bean and cereal flour soup ☞ *Canary Islands*

Dry haricot beans,
    250 g (8 oz; 1 ¹/₂ cups)
Boned loin of pork,
    500 g (1 lb 2 oz)
Lard (or unsmoked bacon),
    150 g (5 oz)
1 onion
2-3 cloves of garlic
2-3 medium-sized potatoes
2 corn-on-the-cob
Bunch of Swiss chards
2 ripe tomatoes
1 gourgette
Bunch of cress
Gofio (see insert)
Fresh coriander and parsley
Salt and pepper
Olive oil

Serves: 4	
Preparation: 25'+4-5h	
Cooking: 1h 30'	
Difficulty: ●●●	
Flavour: ●●	
Kcal (per serving) 1171	
Proteins (per serving): 47	
Fats (per serving): 65	
Nutritional value: ●●●	

1 As usual, soak the beans for about 4-5 hours before starting cooking. After soaking, drain them and put them in a large casserole together with the pork and the lard; cover with cold water, bring to the boil, lower the heat and simmer for about half an hour. Rinse and prepare the chards, cress and gourgette into pieces and add to the casserole. Add salt and pepper to taste.

2 Rinse the corn-on-the-cob, remove the kernels and add them to the soup along with the peeled and diced potatoes. Simmer until all vegetables are cooked (about half an hour), then remove the meat and lard with a draining spoon and arrange on a serving dish, along with the drained vegetables, and keep in a warm place. Filter the cooking liquid.

3 Peel and chop the onion; stew it gently in a casserole (preferable earthenware) with 3-4 tablespoons of oil, adding the garlic and the chopped tomatoes without their seeds. Simmer until everything is tender and soft.

4 Add 3-4 tablespoons of *gofio* and pour in the filtered broth; allow the flavours to combine for 5-6 minutes, or until the liquid has reached boiling point again. Remove from the heat and serve the soup garnished with sprigs of coriander and parsley. The meat and vegetables are served as a second course.

One of the windmills in Tiagua, in the heart of Lanzarote (Canary Islands).

Gofio, *a typical ingredient of Canary Island cooking, is a mixture of toasted cereals such as maize, wheat, barley, etc. It can also be found on the Spanish continent in delicatessens and shops selling biological products. As an alternative, maize flour (polenta flour) can be used after toasting it in a very hot, ungreased skillet.*

SOPA DE MEJILLONES

Mussel soup ☛ *Catalonia*

Mussels, 1 Kg (2 1/4 lb)
1 onion
3-4 ripe tomatoes
3 cloves of garlic
Parsley
Ground cinnamon
Aniseed liqueur or brandy
Slices of toasted farmhouse
  bread (served with the soup)
Salt and pepper
Olive oil

Serves: 4	
Preparation: 30'	
Cooking: 30'	
Difficulty: ● ● ●	
Flavour: ● ●	
Kcal (per serving) 435	
Proteins (per serving): 16	
Fats (per serving): 12	
Nutritional value: ● ●	

Scrub the mussels and remove the 'whiskers'; rinse and place in a pan with a lid; cover with cold water and open the valves over intense heat. As soon as they have opened, remove the pan from the heat; remove the mussels from the shells (which must be discarded) and save the cooking liquid. Chop the onion and stew it gently in 3-4 tablespoons of oil in an earthenware casserole; add the chopped tomatoes (without seeds) and allow the flavours to blend for about a quarter of an hour. Press the tomatoes with the back of a wooden spoon to make a dense sauce. Add the peeled and crushed garlic, the chopped sprig of parsley, a pinch of salt and pepper, a pinch of ground cinnamon, then a small glass of the liqueur. Add the filtered cooking liquid from the mussels, bring to the boil and reduce the soup for a few minutes, stirring all the time. Lower the heat to minimum and add the mussels. After about 4-5 minutes, remove from the heat and serve the soup garnished with chopped parsley and accompanied with the toasted bread.

Meat, POULTRY AND GAME

What do you prefer?
Roasts, braised meat, pastry pies,
a country-style rabbit casserole
with fine herbs,
or a delicious game stew?
The aromas, flavours,
images and colours that make
up Spanish cuisine depict a portrait
of culinary art at its best,
like one of Arcimboldo's famous
paintings.

3

ASADO DE CERDO
A LA CATALANA

Oven-roasted fillet of pork ☞ *Catalonia*

Boned saddle of pork,
  1 Kg (2 1/4 lb)
1 onion
1 stalk of celery
3 cloves of garlic
Cinnamon
2 cloves
Bay leaf, oregano, parsley,
  thyme
Dry Jerez wine
  (Xeres or Sherry)
Salt and freshly ground pepper
Lard, 25 g (1 oz; 2 tbsp)

Serves: 4	
Preparation: 15' +1h	
Cooking: 1h 40'	
Difficulty: ● ●	
Flavour: ● ●	
Kcal (per serving) 333	
Proteins (per serving): 33	
Fats (per serving): 14	
Nutritional value: ● ●	

Pound the peeled garlic to obtain a paste and rub this all over the pork bound with string. Leave the meat to stand on a plate for about one hour then brown it on low heat in an ovenproof earthenware casserole with the melted lard, turning it over now and then to brown evenly on all sides. After rinsing the vegetables, chop the onion and cut the celery into tiny pieces, and add them to the casserole with 2 bay leaves, a sprig each of thyme, oregano and parsley, a small piece of cinnamon, the cloves, and a generous dusting of freshly ground pepper. Put the casserole in the oven heated to 220°C (410°F) for 5 minutes then lower the heat to 180°C (350°F); pour a glass of the wine over the meat and continue cooking for about 1 1/2 hours. Every now and then, check to see that the meat does not dry out and, in this case, baste it with its juice or if necessary, add a few tablespoons of hot water. Taste for salt. When the meat is done, remove from the oven and allow it to stand for a few minutes; remove the string and serve it sliced, with its own gravy (skimmed of fat) in a sauceboat. The best vegetables to serve with it? Potatoes, spinach or turnip tops.

CHULETAS DE CERDO

Marinated pork chops ☞ *Madrid*

Spread the chops side by side at the bottom of a dish and marinate them with the crushed cloves of garlic, one bay leaf torn into pieces, leaves of sprigs of parsley and thyme, half a teaspoon of ground pimiento, a pinch of salt and pepper, half a glass of wine, and 3-4 tablespoons of oil. Marinate for about two hours, turning the chops over now and then.
Put them, still side by side, in a greased ovenproof dish and bake in the oven heated to 180°C (350°F) for about 30 minutes, basting them now and then with the marinade liquid.
Serve with boiled spinach or Swiss chards dressed in lemon juice and oil.

4 pork chops on the bone,
   1 kg total (2 1/4 lb)
3-4 cloves of garlic
Bay leaf, parsley and thyme
Ground pimiento
Red wine
Boiled spinach or Swiss chards
   dressed in lemon
   (as accompaniment)
Salt and pepper
Olivo oil

Serves:	4
Preparation:	10'+2h
Cooking:	30'
Difficulty:	●
Flavour:	● ● ●
Kcal (per serving)	460
Proteins (per serving):	40
Fats (per serving):	22
Nutritional value:	● ●

EMPANADA GALLEGA

Pork pie ☞ *Galicia*

Lean loin of pork, 300 g (10 oz)
2 whole eggs and 1 yolk
1 sweet green pepper
2 onions
2 cloves of garlic
2-3 ripe tomatoes
Bay leaf, oregano and parsley
2 fresh red pimientos
Ground pimiento
Red wine
Salt and pepper
Olive oil

For the pastry:
Plain flour, 300g
 (12 oz; 2 1/2 cups), plus some
 for the pastry board
Maize flour,
 100 g (4 oz; 3/4 cup)
1 egg
Lard, 100 g (4 oz; 4 tbsp)

Serves:	4
Preparation:	35'+2h
Cooking:	50'
Difficulty:	● ● ●
Flavour:	● ● ●
Kcal (per serving)	999
Proteins (per serving):	35
Fats (per serving):	52
Nutritional value:	● ● ●

1 Rub the meat all over with a teaspoonful of ground pimiento, cut it into small cubes then put it into a bowl with a chopped clove of garlic, a bay leaf, a pinch each of oregano, salt and pepper, one glass of red wine and a few drops of oil. Leave the meat to marinate for about 2 hours, turning the cubes over every now and then.

2 Prepare the pastry: mix both flours together in a large bowl and work in (by hand or with a hand mixer) the lard, the egg and a pinch of salt, adding a little water if necessary to obtain a smooth, firm dough. Leave this to stand for one hour.

3 In the meantime, clean and prepare all the vegetables and boil the eggs for 7 minutes; shell the eggs while still hot. Leaving the herbs attached, remove the meat cubes from the marinade liquid (which must be saved) and fry them in a pan (with a lid) with 4-5 tablespoons of oil. When browned, remove with a draining spoon and leave to dry on kitchen paper.

4 Chop the onions and the other clove of garlic and fry gently in the oil remaining in the pan; add the chopped pepper and tomatoes, the marinade liquid and a sprig of parsley; cover with a lid and simmer slowly until the sauce becomes creamy.

5 Roll out the pastry fairly thick (about 8 mm; 1/5 inch) and divide it into two unequal parts (3/5 and 2/5). Use the larger of the two to line a moderately deep pie dish; keep all the pastry trimmings for decoration. Spread the surface of the pastry at the bottom of the dish with some of the sauce, arrange the pork cubes over this, then the boiled eggs cut into rounds; sprinkle the egg rounds with the chopped fresh pimientos then cover with the remaining sauce.

6 Cover the pie with the other piece of pastry, and make a hole in the middle suitable for containing a cone of greaseproof paper, through which the steam will escape; seal the edges of the two sheets of pastry together and decorate the top with shapes made from the pastry trimmings; brush the surface with the beaten egg yolk. Bake in the oven pre-heated to 200°C (375°F) for 20 minutes and leave to cool slightly before serving. The *empanada* is also delicious cold.

CODORNICES EN ZURRÓN

Oven-baked quails 'in jackets' ☛ *La Rioja*

1 The quails must be cleaned of feathers and entrails, passed over a flame to remove any remaining quills, then rinsed well and dried. Sprinkle a little salt and pepper both inside and outside the quails. Brown them in a casserole (preferable earthenware, with a lid) with 3-4 tablespoons of oil, turning them around to brown all sides. Remove and drain them carefully, saving the oil in the casserole.

2 Rinse the peppers, remove the stems and cut them lengthwise, without cutting right through* (they must form a sort of cradle); scoop out the seeds and fibrous parts. Truss the quails by bending and tying their legs near the breasts; put a quail in each pepper. If necessary, the peppers can be tied with kitchen string so that they snugly hold the quails.

3 Gently fry the chopped onion in the casserole, adding more oil if needed; add the finely chopped garlic, and two tablespoons of flour, stirring quickly to avoid the formation of lumps. Place the filled peppers in the casserole and briefly allow the flavours to blend.

4 Add the cleaned, chopped tomatoes without seeds, a glass of wine, the chopped sprig of parsley, salt and pepper. Cover the casserole with its lid and cook in the oven preheated to 180°C (350°F) for about three-quarters of an hour. When ready, eliminate the string and serve immediately.

In photographs 2, 3 and 4, the peppers have been cut open horizontally: this is simply to illustrate the various steps better.

4 single-portion quails ready
  for cooking, approx. 250 g
  (9-10 oz) each
4 sweet peppers, all the same
  colour (preferably green)
1 onion
2 cloves of garlic
3 ripe tomatoes

Parsley
Plain flour
Dry white wine (1 glass)
Salt and freshly ground pepper
Olive oil

Serves: 4		
Preparation: 20'		
Cooking: 1h		
Difficulty: ● ●		
Flavour: ● ●		
Kcal (per serving) 425		
Proteins (per serving): 41		
Fats (per serving): 16		
Nutritional value: ● ●		

| 1 rabbit ready for cooking, with its liver, approx.1. 3 Kg (2 ³/₄ lb) |
| 1 onion |
| 4 cloves of garlic |
| 1 sweet pepper |
| 2-3 ripe tomatoes |
| Wild fennel (a small bunch of fronds) |
| Bay leaf |
| Ground pimiento |
| Dry white wine |
| Salt |
| Olive oil |

Serves: 4
Preparation: 20'
Cooking: 1h
Difficulty: ● ●
Flavour: ● ● ●
Kcal (per serving) 504
Proteins (per serving): 57
Fats (per serving): 20
Nutritional value: ● ●

CONEJO AL HINOJO

Rabbit with wild fennel ☛ *Canary Islands*

1 Rinse and dry the rabbit, then cut it into 10-12 pieces (without the head). Roughly chop the onion and fry it gently in an earthenware casserole, with a lid, with 5-6 tablespoons of oil, adding the chopped pepper and tomatoes without seeds and fibrous parts. Simmer slowly for 10 minutes, then add the peeled garlic. When the garlic starts to turn golden, add the rabbit, a bay leaf and a teaspoon of ground pimiento. Brown the rabbit over intense heat, turning the pieces over so that all parts are browned evenly.

2 Pour a glass of white wine over the rabbit and allow it to evaporate; add salt to taste and a few fronds of wild fennel. Add enough hot water to just cover the rabbit, put the lid back on and bring to the boil; remove the scum off the surface of the liquid, lower the flame and simmer for about 40 minutes. Take the lid off for the last 5-6 minutes of the cooking time to reduce the sauce (which will be served with the rabbit), and check for salt.

CONEJO AL ESTILO TARRACONENSE

Rabbit and chocolate casserole *Catalonia*

1 Rinse and dry the rabbit and cut it into about twenty small pieces (eliminate the head): brown these pieces and the liver evenly in an earthenware casserole with 6 table-spoons of oil. As soon as the rabbit is browned, remove the liver (keep it to one side) and add the chopped onion. When the onion has become soft, add the chopped tomatoes (without seeds); stew a few minutes to let the flavours blend, stirring all the time, then add one and a half glasses of wine, the bouquet garni, a teaspoon of fennel seeds, salt and pepper, and a little grated nutmeg. Cover the casserole, lower the heat to minimum and simmer for about 30 minutes.

2 In the meantime, peel the pota-toes (or if they are new, rub them well under running water but do not remove the skins) and cook them in slightly salted boiling water for about 5 minutes; drain them and cut them in half (or if they are very small, leave them whole). Toast a table-spoon of flour by sprinkling it over the bottom of a dry, ungreased pan on low heat, gently shaking the pan until the flour becomes a nutty colour. Pound the liver in a mortar (or in a food mixer) with a pinch of saffron, the dry pimiento without its seeds, the garlic, the chocolate and the toasted flour. Dilute this paste with half a glass of warm water and add it to the rabbit in the casserole. Add the potatoes and mix gently. Put the lid back on the casserole and simmer for a further 20 minutes, until the rabbit meat is tender. Remove the bouquet garni and serve the rabbit sprinkled with chopped parsley.

1 rabbit (with its liver) ready for cooking, about 1.3 Kg (2 ³/₄ lb)
New potatoes, 500 g (1 lb 2 oz)
1 onion
2-3 ripe tomatoes
2 cloves of garlic
Bouquet garni, tied (bay leaf, parsley, thyme and rosemary)
Sprig of parsley
Nutmeg
Fennel seeds
Saffron
1 dry red pimiento
1 piece of dark chocolate (or unsweetened cocoa powder), 20 g (1 oz)
Plain flour
Red wine
Salt and pepper
Olive oil

Serves: 4
Preparation: 25'
Cooking: 1h ca.
Difficulty: ● ●
Flavour: ● ● ●
Kcal (per serving) 587
Proteins (per serving): 61
Fats (per serving): 21
Nutritional value: ● ●

HORNAZO CASTELLANO

Roll of lamb in vine leaves ☛ *Castile and León*

Minced lamb, 700 g (1 lb 10 oz)
Cured raw ham, 50 g (2 oz)
Lard (or unsmoked bacon),
   50 g (2 oz)
Vine leaves (can be bought),
   approx. 20
1 onion
2 slices of farmhouse bread,
   without crusts
2 eggs
Plain flour, 50 g (2 oz)
Oregano, thyme
Ground cinnamon, nutmeg
Dry white wine
Lettuce (for accompaniment)
Salt and pepper
Olive oil

Serves:	4
Preparation:	25'+15'
Cooking:	1h ca.
Difficulty:	●●
Flavour:	●●●
Kcal (per serving)	712
Proteins (per serving):	45
Fats (per serving):	35
Nutritional value:	●●●

1 Fifteen minutes before starting the preparations, soak the bread in a cup with the wine. If fresh vine leaves are being used, rinse them accurately to eliminate all traces of pesticide, then blanch them for one minute in slightly salted boiling water, remove them and drain them well. Eliminate the stalks. Mix the minced lamb in a bowl with the finely chopped lard and ham; add the bread (squeezed of the wine, which must be kept), salt, pepper, a little grated nutmeg and a pinch of cinnamon.

2 Spread the wine leaves out on a sheet of kitchen foil, or grease-proof paper, and turn in the borders of the foil to obtain a rectangle. Distribute the lamb mixture over the leaves so that a couple of centimetres (just over an inch) are free around all four edges.

3 With the aid of the underlying foil (which will be eliminated), roll up the 'carpet' of leaves and mixture, to obtain a firm roll, which will then be tied with kitchen string. Gently dip the roll in the beaten egg (turning it around so that it becomes completely coated) then in the flour in a large plate or tray. Shake off any excess flour.

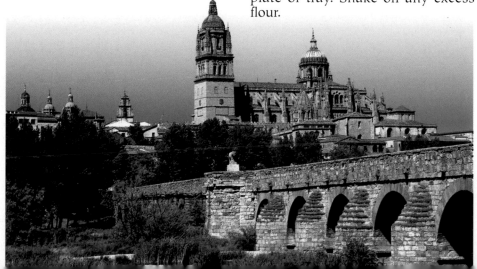

The Roman bridge and the New Cathedral in Salamanca, standing next to the Old Cathedral. The city stands on the right banks of the River Tormes.

4 Put the roll in an ovenproof dish with 6-7 tablespoons of oil, brown it over intense heat, turning it over gently so that it browns evenly all over. Remove from the heat and add the chopped onion, the oregano and thyme, and the wine kept from the bread (add more wine to this so that there is about 4 cm - about 2 ¹/₂ inches - in the glass). Put the roll in the oven pre-heated to 180°C (350°F) for one hour, basting it with its own gravy every now and then. When cooked, remove from the oven, eliminate the string and serve sliced with a salad.

CALDERETA DE CORDERO

Spicy stewed lamb ☞ *Estremadura*

Boned lamb (leg or shoulder),
   approx. 7-800 g (1 lb 10 oz)
1 onion
1 head of garlic, roasted
2 ripe tomatoes
3-4 fresh green pimientos
Bouquet garni, tied
   (bay leaf, parsley, thyme)
Caraway seeds and 1 clove
Ground pimiento
1 slice farmhouse bread
   (without crust)
Salt
Olive oil

Serves: 4	
Preparation: 20'	
Cooking: 1h ca.	
Difficulty: ● ●	
Flavour: ● ● ●	
Kcal (per serving) 339	
Proteins (per serving): 34	
Fats (per serving): 13	
Nutritional value: ● ●	

1 Clean and prepare the vegetables as usual, eliminating the seeds and fibrous parts of the tomatoes and green pimientos. Place the whole head of garlic under the grill, turning it over now and then to roast it evenly. The skin of the garlic should become dark brown, almost black, and crinkled; after about ten minutes, remove the garlic from the grill, separate the cloves and peel them. Cut the lamb into bite-size cubes, place them in an earthenware casserole (with lid) and pour in sufficient water to cover the meat. Bring to the boil over high heat, then lower the heat to minimum; add the onion and tomatoes cut into wedges, the green pimientos cut lengthwise, the roasted and skinned cloves of garlic, the bouquet garni, a pinch of salt and 5-6 tablespoons of oil. Cover the casserole and simmer slowly for about 45 minutes, or until the meat is tender.

2 In the meantime, put the slice of bread to soak in water. About ten minutes before the stew is ready, pound in a mortar (or food mixer) half a teaspoon of caraway seeds, the clove and the soaked bread, squeezed (but keep the water); add a teaspoon of ground pimiento and dilute the paste obtained with a little of the water used for soaking the bread, then stir this paste into the lamb stew. Remove the bouquet garni and serve immediately.

CABRITO AL SALMOREJO

Marinated kid ☛ *Canary Islands*

1 About half an hour before starting to prepare the meal, soak the *ñoras* in warm water; thereafter, squeeze them, eliminate the seeds and pound them in a mortar (or food mixer) with the peeled garlic, the leaves from a sprig of oregano and thyme, half a teaspoon of ground pimiento, salt and pepper. Put this paste into a bowl, dilute it with 3-4 tablespoons of vinegar, stir, then rub this mixture all over the kid meat, cover and leave it to marinate for at least 8 hours. At the end of this time, drain the meat, scraping off all the marinade (both the paste and its liquid are to be saved).

2 Cut the meat into bite-size pieces, brown them in an earthenware casserole with 5-6 tablespoons of oil; cover the pot, lower the heat to mini-mum and simmer for at least half an hour until the meat is tender (if necessary, add one or two tablespoons of hot water during the cooking to keep the meat moist). Put the pieces of meat into a serving dish and keep in a warm place. Add the *salmorejo*, the solid and liquid marinade saved before, to the oil remaining in the casserole, cook over intense heat for about 5 minutes, then pour this sauce over the pieces of meat and serve with *papas arrugadas*. How many? About 5-6 each person.

Ñoras are dried sweet peppers, with a flavour that is subtle rather than hot, shaped like little bells and usually dark red, almost purple in colour. If these cannot be found, a couple of teaspoons of sweet paprika powder may be used.

Boned kid (shoulder or saddle), approx. 7-800 g (1 lb 10 oz)
2 *ñoras* (see below)
1 clove of garlic
Ground pimiento
Oregano and thyme
Papas arrugadas (as accompaniment, see recipe page 110)
Vinegar
Salt and pepper
Olive oil

Serves:	4
Preparation:	20'+8h 30'
Cooking:	40'
Difficulty:	●●
Flavour:	●●●
Kcal (per serving):	265
Proteins (per serving):	29
Fats (per serving):	16
Nutritional value:	●

JABALÍ A LA MONTAÑESA

Marinated wild boar ☛ *Cantabria*

1 The evening before preparing this dish, clean and prepare all the vegetables required for the marinade. Cut the wild boar meat into even, bite-size pieces and put them in a bowl with the carrot and leek cut into thin rounds, the bouquet garni, 3-4 juniper berries, 3-4 peppercorns, the crushed garlic clove and a teaspoon of sugar; pour one and a half glasses of wine and 4-5 tablespoons of oil over it all. Mix and leave over night, even for 24 hours, turning the pieces of meat over every now and then.

Lean wild boar (or fallow deer), 7-800 g (1 lb 10 oz)
Lard, 50 g (2 oz)
Jamón serrano (see below), 50 g (2 oz)
4-5 spring onions
Button mushrooms, cultivated, 150 g (6 oz)
Tomato purée, 100 g (4 oz)
Plain flour
Chicken or vegetable broth (made with bouillon cubes)
Olive oil
For the marinade:
1 carrot
Half a leek
1 clove of garlic
Bouquet garni, tied (bay leaf, mint, parsley, rosemary, thyme)
Juniper berries
Peppercorns
Sugar
Red wine
Olive oil

Serves: 4	
Preparation:	25'+12h
Cooking:	1h 40'
Difficulty:	●●
Flavour:	●●
Kcal (per serving):	782
Proteins (per serving):	38
Fats (per serving):	53
Nutritional value:	●●●

2 Prepare all the other vegetables in the recipe, cleaning the mushrooms accurately. Drain the meat from the marinade and dry it. Save the marinade. Brown the pieces of meat in an earthenware casserole (with lid) with 5-6 tablespoons of oil, turning the meat over frequently so that it browns all over; remove from the casserole, drain and keep in a warm place.

3 Melt the lard in the oil remaining in the casserole; add and brown the diced *jamón serrano*, the whole spring onions and the mushrooms cut into wedges. Put the pieces of wild boar back in the casserole together with the filtered marinade (keep 2 tablespoons for later) and the bouquet garni. Cover and simmer slowly for about 1 hour.

4 In the meantime, heat 2-3 tablespoons of oil in another casserole, gradually add the flour, stirring all the time to avoid lumps, and allow it to colour slowly. Add the broth, the tomato purée and the marinade put aside before. Continue stirring until the sauce thickens. Add this to the meat cooking in the casserole, put the lid back on and simmer slowly for another half-hour, or until the meat is tender. Serve immediately.

Jamón serrano is a cured ham produced in the mountains and is a delicacy the Iberian Peninsula is proud of; it is salted, briefly kept in brine then aged for 12 to 18 months. If it is made in the traditional manner, from cerdo ibérico, *the Spanish black-skinned pigs, the ham should weigh about 6-8 kilos (13-18 lb). Besides being delicious sliced and served as it is, this ham is very often used in cooking. If this type cannot be found, then a good, lean Italian prosciutto, preferably the mild Tuscan type, can be used.*

LIEBRE ESTOFADA A LA CASTELLANA

Hare stew ☞ *Castile and León*

1 hare (preferably young),
   ready for use, 1.3 - 1.5 Kg
   (2 3/4 - 3 lb)
Dry white Spanish beans (butter
   beans), 200 g (1/2 lb)
1 onion
2 cloves of garlic
2-3 fresh green pimientos
Bouquet garni, tied (bay leaf,
   parsley, thyme) plus 1 bay
   leaf
Cinnamon (small piece)
1 dry red pimiento
Dry white wine
Red wine vinegar
Salt and pepper
Olive oil

Serves: 4	
Preparation: 20'+4-5h	
Cooking: 30'	
Difficulty: ●●	
Flavour: ●●	
Kcal (per serving): 630	
Proteins (per serving): 49	
Fats (per serving): 28	
Nutritional value: ●●	

1 About 4-5 hours before starting to prepare the stew, soak the beans in plenty of water. The hare should be ready for cooking (skinned, head and paws cut off, and entrails removed). Cut it into approx. a dozen pieces, put into a bowl, sprinkle with salt and pepper, and a little wine mixed with water. When soaked, put the beans in a casserole and cover with cold water, add a quarter of the onion cut into thin strips, a bay leaf and a pinch of salt. Cover the casserole and slowly bring to the boil; lower the heat and simmer gently for about one hour. In the meantime, prepare all the vegetables, eliminating the seeds of both the fresh green pimientos and the dry red pimiento.

2 Put the pieces of hare into a large earthenware casserole (with lid) and add the rest of the onion, roughly chopped, the peeled and sliced cloves of garlic, the diced green pimientos, the crumbled dry red pimiento, the bouquet garni, a full glass of wine, 2-3 tablespoons of vinegar, 4-5 tablespoons of oil and a pinch of salt. Bring slowly to the boil, lower the heat to minimum, put the lid on the casserole and simmer for about one hour, adding some of the liquid from the cooked beans every time the food absorbs the liquid. Fifteen minutes before the cooking time is up, add the cooked beans, put the lid back on and finish cooking. Allow the stew to cool slightly before serving.

PATO A LA SEVILLANA

Duck with citrus fruit ☞ *Andalusia*

1 The duck must be ready for use (feathers plucked, entrails, fat and glands removed, passed over a flame to remove residual quills, rinsed and dried). Cut it into a dozen or so pieces and brown them in a large casserole (preferably earthenware with a lid) with 6 tablespoons of oil and the onion sliced into thin strips. When the meat is thoroughly browned, remove it from the casserole and keep in a warm place. Skim the excess fat from the casserole. Put a tablespoon of flour into the casserole, let it brown over moderate heat, and then pour in the wine, blending it into the sauce that has formed, stirring all the time.

2 Put the pieces of duck back into the casserole together with the orange (rinsed, separated into segments but without the peel), a sprig of parsley, a bay leaf, the cleaned carrot sliced into rounds, salt and pepper. Add the vegetable broth to almost completely cover the pieces of duck, cover the casserole and simmer slowly for about one hour and 20 minutes. At the end of the cooking time, check that the duck is tender and moist, transfer it to a serving dish and keep in a warm place. Filter the gravy through a sieve and pour it back into the casserole together with the pitted, chopped olives, allowing the flavours to combine over intense heat. Serve this olive sauce beside the duck on the dish.

1 barnyard duck, ready for use, approx. 1.5 Kg (3 lb 6 oz)
1 onion
1 carrot
1 bitter orange (Seville orange), or half a sweet orange and half a lemon
Green olives in brine, 180 g (8 oz)
Bay leaf, sprig of parsley
Plain flour
Vegetable broth (made from bouillon cubes), approx. 1 litre (1 $^1/_2$ pt)
Dry white wine, half a litre ($^3/_4$ pt)
Salt and pepper
Olive oil

Serves:	4-6
Preparation:	25'
Cooking:	1h 40'
Difficulty:	● ●
Flavour:	● ●
Kcal (per serving):	662
Proteins (per serving):	50
Fats (per serving):	30
Nutritional value:	● ● ●

PAELLA A LA VALENCIANA

Valencia paella ☞ *Eastern regions*

1 chicken, ready for use,
   1.2 Kg (2 3/4 lb)
Risotto rice,
   700 g (1 1/2 lb; 3 3/4 cups)
Lean pork, 250 g (10 oz)
6-8 scampi
Fresh clams, 500 g (1 lb 2 oz)
Shelled peas (even frozen),
   300 g (12 oz)
4-5 ripe tomatoes
2 sweet peppers
1 onion
4-5 cloves of garlic
Bay leaf
Saffron
1 lemon
Ground pimiento
Chicken broth, approx. 1 litre
   (1 2/3 pt)
Salt, fresh ground pepper
Olive oil

Serves: 6	
Preparation: 25'	
Cooking: 1h ca.	
Difficulty: ● ●	
Flavour: ● ● ●	
Kcal (per serving): 1107	
Proteins (per serving): 59	
Fats (per serving): 44	
Nutritional value: ● ●	

1 Before starting, roast the peppers under the grill in the oven for about ten minutes, turning them around every now and then, so that they can be skinned easily; remove the stalks, seeds and fibrous parts, then cut into strips. Clean the tomatoes, remove the seeds and chop. Peel the cloves of garlic and the onion and chop finely all together. At this point, cut the chicken into about a dozen pieces and brown in the typical *paellera* (or in another large pan) with 6-7 tablespoons of oil, and a pinch of salt and pepper; when all pieces are golden-brown, remove from the pan and keep in a warm place.

2 Cut the pork into bite-size pieces and brown it in the pan together with the clams (to open them) and the rinsed scampi (do not dry them beforehand). When the scampi become pinkish, take them and the other ingredients out, and put them in a warm place; eliminate any clams that have not opened.

3 Put the chopped onion and garlic into the oil left in the pan and stew until soft; add the tomatoes and peas and simmer gently for about 5 minutes. Add a bay leaf, a sachet of saffron, a teaspoon of ground pimiento, salt and freshly ground pepper; stir well to combine all the flavours. Add the rice, allow it to absorb the sauce for a couple of minutes, then pour in the boiling hot broth; bring back to the boil, lower the heat and simmer for 20 minutes, until the rice has absorbed all the liquid; check for salt. At this point, add the strips of roasted peppers, mix, and then put the chicken and pork pieces, the scampi, and the clams in their shells, all on top of the rice. Cover the *paellera* with kitchen foil and put in the oven pre-heated to 180°C (350°F) for fifteen minutes. Serve in the paellera with wedges of lemon in a separate dish.

The paella, known the world over, takes its name from the typical paellera (a large, not too deep, two-handled pan) traditionally used for cooking this famous, delicious all-in-one dish. It appears to have been originally a fairly humble dish, one made from various leftovers in the enormous pans of noble kitchens and given to the servants.

| 1 chicken, ready for use, approx. 1.2 Kg (2 3/4 lb) |
| 3 spring onions |
| Button mushrooms (cultivated), 100 g (4 oz) |
| Lard, in one piece, 50 g (2 oz) |
| Plain flour |
| Bay leaf, parsley |
| Dry Jerez wine (Xeres or Sherry), 2 dl (4 fl oz) |
| Olive oil |
| Salt and pepper |

Serves:	4
Preparation:	25'
Cooking:	40' ca.
Difficulty:	● ●
Flavour:	● ●
Kcal (per serving):	999
Proteins (per serving):	44
Fats (per serving):	64
Nutritional value:	● ● ●

POLLO AL JEREZ

Chicken in Jerez wine ☛ *Andalusia*

1 The chicken must be already plucked, entrails removed, passed over a flame to eliminate quills, rinsed and dried; cut it into 10-12 pieces and rub a little salt and pepper over them. Brown the chicken pieces in a pan with 5 tablespoons of oil until they are golden-brown; remove them to a casserole and keep in a warm place. Cut the spring onions into rings and dice the lard; gently stew these in the oil left in the pan. Stir in a tablespoon of flour and, gradually, a full glass of wine; toss over intense heat for one minute, stirring all the time.

2 Put this sauce into the casserole containing the chicken; add a bay leaf, check for salt and bring to the boil. Lower the heat, cover the casserole and simmer very gently for about half an hour, adding a little hot water whenever necessary. In the meantime, rinse and slice the mushrooms into wedges and toss them in a pan with 3-4 tablespoons of olive oil; add them to the chicken casserole about 4-5 minutes before the end of cooking time. Transfer the chicken and all its sauce to a serving dish and serve hot with a sprinkling of freshly chopped parsley over it.

POLLO EMBARRADO

Spicy chicken casserole ☛ *Canary Islands*

1 As usual, the chicken must be prepared beforehand: plucked, entrails removed, passed over a flame to eliminate residual quills, rinsed and dried. Make a paste by pounding in a mortar (or food mixer) the peeled cloves of garlic, a small handful of coarse salt, 2 tablespoons of ground pimiento and 3 teaspoons of caraway seeds; put the paste in a bowl and dilute it with half a glass of vinegar and a few drops of wine. Rub this paste all over the chicken (inside and out) and leave to stand for one hour.

2 Cut the chicken into 10-12 pieces and brown them in an earthenware casserole with 5-6 tablespoons of oil, turning them over so that they brown evenly all over. Add a glass of wine, lower the heat under the casserole, put the lid on and simmer gently for half an hour. Every now and then, check that the liquid does not dry out; if necessary, add a little hot water, and check for salt. Serve the chicken hot with its sauce and accompany it with potatoes or, better still, *papas arrugadas*.

1

2

1 chicken, ready for use, approx. 1.2 Kg (2 3/4 lb)
1 head of garlic
Caraway seeds
Ground pimiento
Roast new potatoes, or *papas arrugadas* (as accompaniment; see page 110)
Dry white wine
Vinegar
Coarse salt
Olive oil

Serves:	4
Preparation:	15'+1h
Cooking:	35'
Difficulty:	●●
Flavour:	●●
Kcal (per serving):	843
Proteins (per serving):	46
Fats (per serving):	52
Nutritional value:	●●

POLLO EN SAMFAINA

Chicken with aubergines and sweet peppers ☞ *Catalonia*

1 chicken, ready for use, approx. 1.2 Kg (2 ³/4 lb)	
2 aubergines	
2 sweet peppers	
1 gourgette	
1 onion	
3 cloves of garlic	
2 ripe tomatoes	
Bay leaf, parsley and thyme	
Dry white wine	
Salt and pepper	
Lard, 40 g (1 ¹/2 oz)	

Serves:	4-6
Preparation:	20'+30'
Cooking:	50'
Difficulty:	● ●
Flavour:	● ●
Kcal (per serving):	733
Proteins (per serving):	44
Fats (per serving):	49
Nutritional value:	● ●

1 Half an hour before starting the meal, peel and slice the aubergines and put them in a bowl; cover them with salt, and weigh them down with a heavy object so that their bitter flavour 'sweats' out. In the meantime, clean and prepare the peppers, tomatoes and the gourgette. The chicken must be ready for use (plucked, entrails removed, passed over a flame to eliminate residual quills, rinsed and dried); cut it into 10-12 pieces, rub these with salt and pepper and leave to stand for 15 minutes. Rinse the slices of aubergines, dry them well, cut them into cubes and stir-fry them for a couple of minutes in a casserole with a tablespoon of melted lard; add the roughly cut peppers and the diced gourgette and allow the flavours to blend.

2 Melt the remaining lard in another casserole (earthenware this time) and brown the chicken pieces in it with the thinly sliced onion. Add the chopped garlic and tomatoes; stir over intense heat for 2-3 minutes then add a glass (not full) of wine, a bay leaf, a sprig each of thyme and parsley, salt and pepper. Lower the heat, cover the casserole and simmer very gently for about half an hour. At the end of this time, take the lid off, increase the heat to medium, add the aubergines, peppers and gourgette and reduce the liquid for about ten minutes. Serve immediately.

MAR I TERRA

Chicken with lobster and chocolate ☞ *Catalonia*

1 Toast the almonds and hazelnuts for about ten minutes in the oven pre-heated to 200°C (375°F). As usual, the chicken must be ready for use (plucked, entrails removed, passed over a flame to eliminate residual quills, rinsed and dried); cut it into small pieces and rub these with a mixture of salt, pepper and a pinch of cinnamon, shaking off the excess. Brown the chicken pieces and the cleaned liver in 4-5 tablespoons of oil in an earthenware casserole (with lid) until golden-brown. Remove the liver and add the chopped onion and leek; allow these to stew slowly then add the bouquet garni, the grated orange peel, the rinsed and chopped tomatoes (without seeds), and two glasses of wine. Lower the heat under the casserole and gently simmer until the liquid has reduced to half its volume (about 15 minutes); add two tablespoons of breadcrumbs, sufficient hot water to cover the pieces of chicken, put the lid on the casserole and gently simmer for a further 15 minutes.

2 In the meantime, pound in a mortar (or in a food mixer) the almonds, hazelnuts, garlic, chicken liver and the crumbled chocolate; add a pinch of saffron to this paste and dilute it with a drop of hot water. Rinse and prepare the lobster: remove the shell and cut the meat into 8-10 pieces (not too thick) and briefly fry in a little oil in a pan, then add to the chicken in the casserole. Add the paste from the mortar and mix gently to combine all the flavours; remove from the heat. After a few minutes, eliminate the bouquet garni, sprinkle with chopped parsley and serve.

1 chicken (with liver), approx. 1.2 Kg (2 3/4 lb)
1 lobster (or crawfish), approx. 1 Kg (2 lb 2 oz)
1 onion
2-3 ripe tomatoes
2 cloves of garlic
A piece of leek
Shelled and peeled almonds and hazelnuts (a small handful)
Bouquet garni, tied (bay leaf, oregano, parsley, thyme) plus an extra sprig of parsley
Peel of half an orange
Cinnamon and saffron
Dark chocolate (or unsweetened cocoa), 20 g (1 oz)
Dry white wine
Dry breadcrumbs
Salt and pepper
Olive oil

Serves:	6-8
Preparation:	20′
Cooking:	45′+10′
Difficulty:	● ●
Flavour:	● ●
Kcal (per serving):	673
Proteins (per serving):	46
Fats (per serving):	40
Nutritional value:	● ●

PASTEL A LA MURCIANA

Mixed meat pie ☞ *Murcia*

1 Put 250 g (10 oz; 2 cups) of flour into a basin, add the yeast diluted with lukewarm water, the lard, the egg white and a pinch of salt; knead by hand or with a hand-mixer for about 15 minutes. Shape the dough into a ball, cover it with a clean cloth and leave it to rise for a couple of hours in a warm place. In the meantime, use the remaining flour and the butter to prepare the flaky pastry as illustrated on page 117 (adapting the recipe to the amounts used here). Hard-boil the eggs for 7 minutes, remove from the water, allow them to cool, then shell them.

2 Chop the onion and the garlic together and fry them gently in a casserole with 5-6 tablespoons of oil; add the chicken cut into about a dozen pieces, and the beef cut into bite-size pieces, and brown evenly. Add a chopped sprig of parsley, the juice of the lemon, salt and pepper. Pour in sufficient water to cover the chicken, bring to the boil, cover the casserole, lower the heat to minimum and simmer gently for just under 30 minutes. In the meantime, rinse the brain in cold running water then blanch it in slightly salted water for about 3-4 minutes. When the chicken is cooked, remove the pieces from the casserole, eliminate the skin and bones and cut the meat into small cubes; put these back into the casserole containing the beef and add the cubed brain.

3 Roll out the shortcrust pastry (the one without butter) and line an ovenproof pie dish with it; fill with the mixture of meats, level out the surface, add the slices of *chorizo* and rounds of boiled eggs. Roll out the flaky pastry and use it to cover the pie, sealing the edges well and using the trimmings for decorating the top. Remember to put a cone of greaseproof paper in a hole in the middle to allow the steam to escape.

For the two types of pastries:
Plain flour, 375 g (14 oz; 2 ³/4 cups), plus extra for the pastry board
White of one egg
Salt
Baker's yeast, 15 g (¹/2 oz)
Lard, 30 g (1 oz)
Butter, 125 g (¹/4 lb; ²/3 cup)

1 chicken, ready for use, 1.2 Kg (2 ³/4 lb)
Leftover roast beef (or raw), 200 g (8 oz)
1 lamb brain, ready for use
Chorizo (see insert), 150 g (5-6 oz)
2 eggs
1 onion
1 clove of garlic
Parsley
1 lemon
Salt and pepper
Olive oil

Serves:	4-6
Preparation:	50'+2h
Cooking:	1h 15'
Difficulty:	●●●
Flavour:	●●
Kcal (per serving):	1397
Proteins (per serving):	64
Fats (per serving):	88
Nutritional value:	●●●

The most commonly found Iberian cured meat is the famous chorizo, *a delicious salami made of minced fat and lean pork (sometimes mixed with beef), and plenty of spices and flavouring such as ground pimiento (more or less* caliente, *hot), garlic, pepper, and so on; rather like the spiced sausages found in Southern Italy. There are several types on the market, all with different coloured labels; the best types for* tapas *and bocadillos are those that have matured longer (up to 3 months) whereas, for cooking, the fresher ones are recommended.*

4 Pre-heat the oven to 220°C (410°F) and bake the *pastel* for 15 minutes; remove it from the oven, and brush the surface with beaten egg yolk. Lower the heat to 180°C (350°F) and continue baking the *pastel* for a further 20 minutes. If you are not partial to lamb brain, use a bigger chicken or a greater quantity of beef.

COCIDO MADRILEÑO

Mixed boiled meats ☞ *Madrid*

If you want to follow the tradition, you can filter the cocido broth and cook fideos (see page 28) or rice in it and serve it as a soup.

1 Four or five hours before starting, soak the chickpeas in water. Drain them and put them in a large casserole with the chicken and beef cut into pieces, the diced lard and *chorizo*, the ham bone, the trimmed carrot and celery and the onion with the clove in it. Cover with plenty of cold water and bring to the boil; lower the heat, cover with a lid and simmer for about one and a half hours.

2 Peel the potatoes and cut them into rounds; trim and rinse the cabbage, eliminating the core, and cut it into eight wedges. Add these ingredients to the meat in the casserole with salt to taste; cover once more and simmer for a further half-hour.

3 Remove from the heat and when the broth is no longer boiling, extract the cabbage and potatoes with a draining spoon; drain well. Slowly fry the peeled garlic cloves (cut into two lengthwise) with 5-6 tablespoons of oil in a pan; remove the cloves and use this oil to stir-fry the cabbage and potatoes rapidly (they must not brown). Drain the vegetables of the oil and serve with the meats (chicken, beef, lard and *chorizo*) in a serving dish, eliminating the ham bone.

A quarter of a chicken,
   ready for use
Lean beef, 250 g (10 oz)
Chorizo, (see page 60),
   100 g (4 oz)
Lard (in one piece),
   100 g (4 oz)
Ham bone
White cabbage, 1 Kg (1 lb 2 oz)
Chickpeas, 250 g (10 oz)
3 potatoes
1 carrot
1 onion speared with one clove
2 cloves of garlic
Salt and pepper
Olive oil

Serves:	4-6
Preparation:	25'+4-5h
Cooking:	2h ca.
Difficulty:	● ●
Flavour:	● ●
Kcal (per serving):	809
Proteins (per serving):	41
Fats (per serving):	49
Nutritional value:	● ●

ROPA VIEJA

Beef leftovers with vegetables
☞ *Castile and León*

Left-over roast (or boiled) beef,
  700 g (1 lb 10 oz)
2 aubergines
1 onion
1 clove of garlic
1 sweet pepper
Plain flour
Tomato purée, 100 g (4 oz)
Chicken or vegetable broth
  (made with bouillon cubes)
Salt and pepper
Olive oil
Coarse salt

Serves:	4-6
Preparation:	20'+30'
Cooking:	35'
Difficulty:	● ●
Flavour:	● ●
Kcal (per serving):	331
Proteins (per serving):	30
Fats (per serving):	14
Nutritional value:	●

1 Peel and slice the aubergines, cover them with coarse salt and put them under a weight in a flat dish for about half an hour to sweat out the bitter flavour. In the meantime, clean the pepper and remove its seeds, then roast it under the grill for about ten minutes, turning it over now and then; skin it and slice it into strips. Rinse and dry the aubergine slices then brown them in a pan with 6-7 tablespoons of oil, turning them around to brown both sides.

2 Gently fry the chopped onion and garlic in the oil left in the pan; gradually add a couple of tablespoons of flour, stirring continuously to avoid the formation of lumps. Add the strips of pepper, the tomato purée, 2-3 ladles of broth, and season with salt and pepper. Allow the flavours to combine, then add the meat and the aubergines cut into strips. Mix and stew gently for about ten minutes then serve immediately.

This is a famous dish which, like many other traditional recipes, was invented to use up leftovers (in fact, the name of the dish means 'old clothes'). Another way of cooking it foresees the addition of cooked chickpeas, as in the cocido *on the previous page.*

ESTOFADO A LA ANDALUZA

Spicy beef stew ☛ *Andalusia*

Lean beef (Pope's eye or other
firm cut), 1Kg (2 ¼ lb)
1 sweet pepper
1 ripe tomato
1 onion
2 carrots
3-4 potatoes
1 head of garlic
Bay leaf and parsley
1 small piece of cinnamon stick
1 clove
Saffron powder
Dry white wine
Salt and peppercorns
Olive oil

Serves:	6-8
Preparation:	25'
Cooking:	1h 30'
Difficulty:	● ●
Flavour:	● ● ●
Kcal (per serving):	469
Proteins (per serving):	36
Fats (per serving):	12
Nutritional value:	●

1 Roast the whole head of garlic for about ten minutes under the grill in the oven (see page 48), turning it over now and then. Separate the cloves and peel them. Rinse and trim the pepper, tomato, carrot and onion. Cut the beef into cubes and gently brown them in a casserole (preferably earthenware with a lid) with 4-5 tablespoons of oil, the pepper cut into strips, the tomato in pieces, the onion in thin slices and the carrots cut into two lengthwise then into small pieces.

2 Pound 6 peppercorns in a mortar with the clove, the roasted garlic and the small piece of cinnamon; when it is the consistency of a paste, add the sachet of saffron. Dilute the paste with a small glass of hot water and pour it into the casserole together with 4-5 tablespoons of oil, half a glass of wine, a bay leaf, chopped parsley (one sprig) and a pinch of salt. Cover the casserole and simmer for about 45 minutes, adding hot water whenever necessary. Add the peeled potatoes cut into rounds (or each round cut in two if they are too big), taste for salt, cover again and simmer for another 20-25 minutes. Serve the *estofado* hot in its earthenware casserole.

Fish, SHELLFISH AND SEAFOOD

*Here we can enjoy the best
of traditional Spanish cooking in a series
of unforgettable dishes, from the Basque
marmitako to the tropical flavour
of Canary Island octopus,
from the multi-coloured zarzuela to the
spicy sword-fish served in Malaga, from
squids cooked in their ink to delicate
cuttlefish cooked with mushrooms.
Enough to make you lose your senses (all
except your sense of taste, of course)...*

4

ATÚN ENCEBOLLADO

Tuna fish with onions ☞ *Basque Counties*

Tuna fish (1 slice),
  700 g (1 lb 10 oz)
4 onions
2 cloves of garlic
Bay leaf and thyme
Ground pimiento
Dry white wine
Vinegar
Salt and pepper
Olive oil

Serves:	4
Preparation:	10'
Cooking:	30'
Difficulty:	●
Flavour:	●●●
Kcal (per serving):	361
Proteins (per serving):	37
Fats (per serving):	15
Nutritional value:	●

Rinse the tuna fish in cold running water until the blood runs out; dry it and pierce it with pieces of garlic, sprinkle with salt, pepper and a pinch of ground pimiento. Peel the onions, cut them into wedges and gently fry them for 3-4 minutes in a pan (preferably earthenware with a lid) with 3-4 tablespoons of oil; when they are golden, remove them and keep to one side. Put the tuna fish in the oil and brown it on both sides, on a very low heat. Add half a bay leaf, a sprig of thyme and a tablespoon of vinegar; put the onions back into the pan and add a glass of wine. Cover the pan and simmer very slowly for 20 minutes. Serve immediately in its own sauce.

BACALAO AL PIL-PIL

Dried cod with pimiento ☛ *Basque Counties*

Cut the cod into pieces without removing the skin; eliminate all bones and any tough parts. Fry the pieces of cod together with the peeled and crushed cloves of garlic in a large frying pan with 8-10 tablespoons of oil; when the garlic becomes golden, remove it with the pieces of cod and half of the oil and keep in a warm place. Slowly cook the finely chopped onions for 5 minutes in the remaining oil; when the onion is transparent, gently put the pieces of cod, side by side with the skin underneath, back into the casserole and sprinkle with a teaspoonful of ground pimiento. Pour in sufficient warm fish broth to almost cover the fish. Cook over a low heat for 15 minutes, shaking the casserole every now and then; when the liquid reaches boiling point, add the garlic (chopped) and oil kept back previously and a pinch of freshly ground pepper. Simmer for another 5 minutes, remove from the heat and drain the cod. Reduce the tasty sauce over intense heat for about 5-6 minutes, pour it over the cod and serve immediately.

Soaked dried cod,
  800 g (1 3/4 lb)
2 onions
6 cloves of garlic
Ground pimiento
Fish broth (made with
  bouillon cubes),
  approx. 1 litre (3/4 pt)
Freshly ground pepper
Olive oil

Serves:	4
Preparation:	10'
Cooking:	35'
Difficulty:	● ●
Flavour:	● ● ●
Kcal (per serving):	357
Proteins (per serving):	47
Fats (per serving):	16
Nutritional value:	●

BACALAO A LA VIZCAÍNA

Dried cod in sweet pepper sauce ☛ *Basque Counties*

1 Thirty minutes before starting, soak the *pimientos choriceros* in cold water. Rinse and dry the fresh peppers, remove the stalks, seeds and fibrous parts; roast them in the oven until the skins are black then skin them and cut into strips. Put the previously soaked cod into a casserole and cover it with cold water, without adding salt. Bring to the boil. As soon as the water boils, switch off the heat and remove the cod; keep the liquid in the casserole. Cut the fish into bite-size pieces, removing all bones and tough parts.

2 Peel and chop the onion and fry it gently in a pan with 5-6 tablespoons of oil; add the tomatoes without their seeds and cut into pieces; allow the flavours to combine over low heat for 10 minutes. Add the *pimientos* squeezed of all water, the fresh red pepper and a couple of full tablespoons of breadcrumbs.

3 Pour in two ladles of the cod cooking liquid and cook the sauce over intense heat for 15 minutes. Add another two ladles of liquid, lower the heat and simmer for half an hour, adding more liquid whenever necessary.

4 When the sauce is cooked, put it first into a liquidiser then pass it through a fine sieve. Spread a thin layer of sauce over the bottom of an earthenware oven dish, arrange the pieces of cod over it then pour the rest of the sauce over them (dilute the sauce with a drop of the liquid if it appears too thick). Distribute the strips of roast pepper over the top and put in the oven (preheated to 200°C; 375°F) for 15 minutes. In the meantime, peel the cloves of garlic, cut into thin slices and fry in 2-3 tablespoons of oil. When the cod is cooked, remove the dish from the oven, distribute the drained slices of garlic over the top and serve immediately.

Soaked dried cod,
   800 g (1 3/4 lb)
10 *pimientos choriceros*
   (see underneath)
2 red sweet peppers
2 ripe tomatoes
1 onion
3 cloves of garlic

1 fresh red pimiento
Dry breadcrumbs
Olive oil

Serves:	4
Preparation:	20'+30'
Cooking:	1h 30'
Difficulty:	● ●
Flavour:	● ● ●
Kcal (per serving):	406
Proteins (per serving):	47
Fats (per serving):	13
Nutritional value:	●

Similar to the ñoras (see page 49), the **pimientos chorizeros** *are sun-dried sweet peppers that must be soaked before use. If they cannot be found, sweet paprika in powder may be used (5-6 teaspoons).*

BESUGO A LA DONOSTIARRA

Grilled schnapper ☞ *Basque Counties*

1 schnapper, approx. 1 Kg
  (2 1/4 lb)
5-6 cloves of garlic
1 lemon
1 fresh red pimiento
Parsley (1 sprig)
Salt
Olive oil

Serves: 4	
Preparation: 10'+1h	
Cooking: 12'	
Difficulty: ●	
Flavour: ● ● ●	
Kcal (per serving): 305	
Proteins (per serving): 44	
Fats (per serving): 12	
Nutritional value: ●	

Remove the scales from the fish, gut it, then rinse and dry it inside and out. Rub a little salt over it, inside and out, leaving it like this for about one hour. Thereafter, put it under the grill in the oven or, better still, barbecue it over glowing coals, turning it over after about 5-6 minutes and brushing it with oil on both sides. Serve the fish accompanied with a sauce made from the chopped garlic fried for 5-6 minutes in half a glass of oil, and when cooked, remove from the heat, add the juice of the lemon then the chopped pimiento and parsley.

BOGAVANTE A LA GALLEGA

Pan-cooked lobster ☛ *Galicia*

1 lobster, 1 - 1.2 Kg (2 ^{1}/$_4$ - 2 ^{1}/$_2$ lb)
1 onion
2 cloves of garlic
1 ripe tomato
Bay leaf
Ground pimiento
Dry white wine
Salt and pepper
Olive oil

Serves: 4	
Preparation: 20′	
Cooking: 25′	
Difficulty:	● ●
Flavour:	● ● ●
Kcal (per serving): 349	
Proteins (per serving): 37	
Fats (per serving): 13	
Nutritional value:	● ●

1 Rinse the lobster, open its shell and remove the meat, eliminating the intestinal part. Cut the meat into even slices about one centimetre (²/₃ inch) thick. Crush the shells of the legs and the claws and extract the flesh. Skin and chop the onion together with the peeled garlic and fry them gently for 5 minutes in a pan (preferably earthenware with a lid) with 4-5 tablespoons of oil. Add the chopped tomato (without seeds) and the flesh from the legs and claws; increase the heat under the pan and stir well, allowing the flavours to blend for 5 minutes.

2 Add the slices of lobster, a bay leaf and a teaspoon of ground pimiento. Stir and add a glass of wine, leaving it to evaporate slightly. Lower the heat to minimum, add salt and pepper to taste, cover and simmer slowly for 12 minutes. Before serving the lobster, cover it with the tomato sauce and allow it to cool for a few minutes.

CALAMARES EN SU TINTA

Squids in their ink ☞ *Basque Counties*

Fishermen in Ondárroa, a small fishing port in the Basque Counties.

1 Clean the squids, eliminating the cartilage, the entrails, the eyes and mouth, and saving 4-5 of the ink sacs. Rinse the squids well, inside and out, and remove the external membrane. Cut off the side fins, separating them from the rest of the body, and chop them together with the tentacles and whatever of the head is left over; mix this with 4-5 tablespoons of breadcrumbs and one finely chopped clove of garlic. Use this mixture to stuff the squid bodies, closing them with a toothpick.

2 Roll the stuffed squids in the flour on a plate, shake off any excess flour then fry them with 5-6 tablespoons of oil in a pan until golden; remove them and put them on kitchen paper to drain and dry. Then put them in a casserole, preferably earthenware.

3 Drain off the oil used for frying the squids and put 4-5 tablespoons of fresh oil in the pan; fry the finely chopped onion and the remaining garlic in this. Add the tomato purée, a bay leaf, the fresh pimiento, a glass of wine, salt and pepper. Allow the sauce to reduce slowly for 5-6 minutes, then pour it over the squids in the casserole.

4 Cover the casserole and slowly simmer for about 30 minutes, adding hot water whenever necessary and tasting for salt. A few minutes before the cooking time is up, break the ink sacs open and drop the contents into a bowl, dilute the ink with a drop of wine, then pour it into the casserole. Mix gently, allow the flavours to combine, then serve immediately sprinkled with chopped parsley.

Squids (medium-small),
  1 Kg (2 1/4 lb)
1 onion
2 cloves of garlic
Tomato purée, 1 dl (4 fl oz)
1 fresh red pimiento
Bay leaf, sprig of parsley
Plain flour, 50 g (2 oz; 5-6 tbsp)

Dry breadcrumbs
Dry white wine
Salt and pepper
Olive oil

Serves:	4
Preparation:	30'
Cooking:	50'
Difficulty:	● ●
Flavour:	● ● ●
Kcal (per serving):	437
Proteins (per serving):	36
Fats (per serving):	15
Nutritional value:	● ●

L'CAP ROIG' CON SALSA DE AJO

Garlic scorpion fish ☛ *Catalonia*

1 scorpion fish,
    approx. 1.2 Kg (2 ^{1}/$_2$ lb)
3-4 cloves of garlic
Fish broth (made with bouillon
    cubes)
Parsley (large sprig)
Dry white wine
Salt
Olive oil

Serves:	4
Preparation:	10'+30'
Cooking:	30'
Difficulty:	●
Flavour:	●●
Kcal (per serving):	347
Proteins (per serving):	38
Fats (per serving):	15
Nutritional value:	●

Prepare the fish by removing the scales (be careful with the sharp fins) and the entrails, then rinse it well inside and out. Rub it all over with salt and leave to stand for about 30 minutes; thereafter, place it in an oiled oven-proof dish and pour a glass of fish broth and half a glass of wine over it. Cook in the oven pre-heated to 180°C (350°F) for just under 30 minutes. Peel the garlic cloves and slice them lengthwise, then fry them until golden in a small pot with half a glass of oil. Remove from the heat, add the chopped parsley. Drain the fish and serve it with the aromatic sauce and slices of lemon.

The tables of cafés and restaurants in front of the Palau del Mar, the site of the Catalonia History Museum (Barcelona).

Mixed fish for soup (dogfish,
   grouper, swallow-fish,
   gurnard, etc.), ready for use,
   approx. 1 Kg (2 $^1/_4$ lb)
2 onions
3 ripe tomatoes
2 sweet peppers
4 cloves of garlic
Bay leaf, parsley, thyme,
   saffron
Salt and freshly ground pepper
Vinegar
Olive oil

Serves:	4
Preparation:	20′
Cooking:	30′
Difficulty:	● ●
Flavour:	● ● ●
Kcal (per serving):	323
Proteins (per serving):	41
Fats (per serving):	13
Nutritional value:	●

ENCEBOLLADO DE PESCADO

Fish and onion casserole ☛ *Canary Islands*

All the fish must be ready for use: scales, entrails, heads, tails and fins removed, and rinsed, dried then cut into pieces. Put these pieces in a casserole and cover them with slightly salted, cold water. Bring slowly to the boil, cook for 8 minutes then switch off the heat and remove and drain the fish. Prepare the onions by chopping them fine and stewing them slowly until tender in an earthenware casserole with 5-6 tablespoons of oil; add the peppers (rinsed, without seeds and fibrous parts, and cut into small pieces), a bay leaf, a sprig each of parsley and thyme, a pinch of saffron, then the tomatoes (without seeds) cut into pieces.

Desertic-like scenery in the Timanfaya National Park, Lanzarote, Canary Islands.

While these ingredients are all gently simmering, pound the peeled garlic in a mortar, then add a pinch of salt and a dash of freshly ground pepper; dilute the paste with a teaspoon of vinegar. Add this mixture to the sauce in the casserole and cook for 2-3 minutes, stirring all the time. At this point add the drained fish, bring back to the boil and cook for 5-6 minutes, stirring with care. Serve immediately.

75

LJIBIAS CON SETAS

Cuttlefish with mushrooms *Catalonia and Eastern regions*

Cuttlefish, 1 Kg (2 $^1/4$ lb)	
Boletus (or chanterelle) mushrooms, 500 g (1 lb 2 oz)	
2 onions	
5 cloves of garlic	
Tomato pulp, 2.5 dl (6 fl oz)	
Shelled, toasted almonds, approx. 12	
1 fresh red pimiento	
Dry white wine	
Salt	
Olive oil	

Serves:	4
Preparation:	25'
Cooking:	1h 10'
Difficulty:	● ●
Flavour:	● ●
Kcal (per serving):	397
Proteins (per serving):	42
Fats (per serving):	14
Nutritional value:	●

1 Prepare the cuttlefish: eliminate the cuttle-bone, entrails, eyes and mouth, and the ink sacs. Rinse them well inside and out, remove the outside membrane then cut the fish into strips. Peel the onions, cut them into thick slices and fry until golden in a casserole (preferably earthenware) with 6-8 table-spoons of oil; add the tomato pulp and the pimiento (left whole) and simmer slowly for about 10 minutes. Add the cuttlefish, and salt to taste, then cover with hot water. Put the lid on the casserole and simmer for about 30 minutes. In the meantime, prepare the mush-rooms by gently scraping off the soil and wiping them with a piece of damp kitchen paper (do not rinse them); cut them into small pieces, add to the cuttlefish, then continue to cook for a further 15 minutes.

2 Toast the almonds in the oven then pound them in a mortar together with the peeled garlic; dilute the paste obtained with half a glass of wine. Add this mixture to the cuttle-fish in the casserole, stir, taste for salt, put the lid back on and finish cooking (about an-other 10 minutes).

MARMITAKO

Tuna fish with potatoes and sweet peppers
☞ *Basque Counties*

Rinse the tuna in cold running water until all the blood runs out; dry it then cut it into bite-size pieces, sprinkle these with the juice of the lemon, salt and pepper and leave to one side. Clean and prepare all the vegetables for use. Gently fry the chopped onion in a pan (with a lid) with 6-7 tablespoons of oil; add the peeled garlic and the pepper cut into strips. Allow the flavours to combine for 5 minutes, then add the chopped tomatoes, the fresh pimiento, a pinch each of salt and pepper and a teaspoon of ground pimiento. Cover the pan and simmer for 10 minutes. In the meantime, peel the potatoes and cut them into small cubes; add these to the sauce in the pan, pour in the wine, then put the lid on once more and simmer for about 20 minutes. At this point, add the tuna fish, stir very gently, then cook for a further 5-6 minutes, with the lid on, and taste for salt. Serve immediately.

Fresh tuna fish (1 slice), 700 g
  (1 lb 10 oz)
Floury potatoes,
  800 g (1 ¾ lb)
1 onion
4 cloves of garlic
2 sweet peppers
4-5 ripe tomatoes
1 fresh red pimiento
Ground pimiento
1 lemon
Dry white wine, 2.5 dl (6 fl oz)
Salt and pepper
Olive oil

Serves: 4-6	
Preparation: 20′	
Cooking: 40′	
Difficulty: ● ●	
Flavour: ● ● ●	
Kcal (per serving): 501	
Proteins (per serving): 32	
Fats (per serving): 14	
Nutritional value: ●	

MERLUZA A LA KOTXKERA

Golden fried cod with asparagus ☞ *Basque Counties*

4 slices of cod, 900 g (2 lb)
2 dozen asparagus
  (preferably small)
Shelled fresh peas, 100 g (4 oz)
6 cloves of garlic
4 eggs
Parsley
Plain flour, 50 g (4 oz; 4 tbsp)
Dry white wine
Salt and pepper
Olive oil

Serves: 4-6	
Preparation: 25'	
Cooking: 50'	
Difficulty: ● ●	
Flavour: ● ●	
Kcal (per serving): 512	
Proteins (per serving): 43	
Fats (per serving): 24	
Nutritional value: ● ●	

1 Rinse the asparagus well, removing all signs of soil. Tie them into a bunch and stand them upright in a deep pot, pour water in until it reaches the beginning of the green part of the stalks and boil for 15 minutes. Remove the asparagus from the pot and rinse them under running cold water under cooled. Untie the bunch then cut off and discard the white parts of the stalks; save the cooking liquid. In the meantime, boil the eggs for 7 minutes, cool them under cold running water, then shell them. Cut the cod slices to remove the central bone, put them back into shape and sprinkle a little salt over them; leave to one side for 15 minutes. Boil the peas in slightly salted water for 7-8 minutes; drain them but do not discard the cooking liquid.

2 Dip the cod slices in flour, coating both sides and shaking them to eliminate any excess flour; fry them until golden on both sides in a casserole with 5 tablespoons of oil.

A spectacular view from the sea in front of San Sebastián, the capital of Guipúzcoa, one of the Basque Counties.

3 Add the chopped garlic and the wine; then gradually add the filtered liquid left over from the peas and the asparagus, and cook over low heat for about 15 minutes until the sauce becomes thick and creamy. To avoid the fish sticking to the bottom of the pan, gently shake the pan from one side to another every now and then, but do not use spoons or other utensils.

4 Add the drained peas and allow the flavours to blend for a few seconds. Serve the slices of cod with the creamy sauce, peas, asparagus tips, rounds of boiled egg and a sprinkling of chopped parsley.

MEJILLONES RELLENOS

Stuffed mussels ☛ *Eastern regions*

Mussels, 1 Kg (2 ¹/₄ lb)	
2 sweet peppers	
1 onion	
1 clove of garlic	
Parsley	
Dry white wine	
Salt and pepper	
Olive oil	

Serves: 4	
Preparation: 25′	
Cooking: 20′	
Difficulty: ●	
Flavour: ●●	
Kcal (per serving): 273	
Proteins (per serving): 19	
Fats (per serving): 13	
Nutritional value: ●	

Scrape the shells of the mussels, remove the 'whiskers' between the valves, and rinse them well but do not dry them. Rinse the peppers, remove the stalks, seeds and fibrous parts; cut the peppers into strips or dice them then stew them slowly for 3-4 minutes in a pan, with the sliced garlic and onion and 3-4 tablespoons of oil.

Add the mussels, a glass of wine and a few sprigs of parsley.

Cover the pan and cook for about ten minutes, until all the mussels have opened.

Remove the pan from the heat; extract the mussels and place them on a serving dish, discarding the empty shell of each one.

Filter the liquid left in the pan; distribute spoonfuls of the ingredients left in the sieve into the mussels in the half shells then pour some of the filtered liquid over them, add a pinch of salt and if desired, a dash of freshly ground pepper.

Serve the mussels at room temperature, sprinkled with chopped parsley. This is a simple dish that is ideal in Summer, but it can also be used as a tasty appetiser, served with an excellent dry white wine brought up from the cellar.

PEZ ESPADA A LA MALAGUEÑA

Swordfish with vegetables ☞ *Andalusia*

Peel the onion and chop it roughly. Rinse the sweet pepper and the tomatoes, eliminate their seeds and fibrous parts and cut them into small pieces.

Put the vegetables in a large pan with the chopped garlic, a bay leaf, the clove, 4-5 peppercorns, 5 tablespoons of oil, then the slightly salted swordfish.

Sauté over medium heat; add a full glass of wine, bring to the boil, cover the pan and simmer for just under 20 minutes, until the fish is cooked. Remove the fish from the pan and place it on a serving dish, sprinkling chopped parsley over it and arranging all the cooked vegetables neatly around it.

Swordfish, one slice, approx. 900 g (2 lb)
1 onion
4-5 cloves of garlic
1 green sweet pepper
2 ripe tomatoes
Bay leaf
2 cloves
Dry white wine
Parsley
Salt and peppercorns
Olive oil

Serves:	4
Preparation:	15'
Cooking:	20'
Difficulty:	●
Flavour:	● ● ●
Kcal (per serving):	430
Proteins (per serving):	49
Fats (per serving):	17
Nutritional value:	●

PULPOS CANARIOS

Octopus and onion casserole ☞ *Canary Islands*

| Octopus (small-medium size), 1 Kg (2 ¼ lb) |
| 2 medium sized onions |
| 3 cloves of garlic |
| Parsley |
| Dry white wine |
| Course salt |
| Vinegar |
| Olive oil |

Serves: 4
Preparation: 20'
Cooking: 45+20'
Difficulty: ● ●
Flavour: ● ●
Kcal (per serving): 308
Proteins (per serving): 28
Fats (per serving): 2
Nutritional value: ●

1 Prepare the octopus by turning the sacs inside out to eliminate the entrails, then remove the 'tooth' and eyes; rinse well, cut into pieces then rub these all over with coarse salt. Put the peeled and sliced garlic and the onions cut into rings into a casserole (preferable earthenware, with a lid); wipe the salt off the pieces of octopus and place them in the casserole with one tablespoon of oil, 2 tablespoons of vinegar and sufficient cold water to cover them.

2 Cover the casserole and slowly bring to the boil over low heat; remove the scum that forms, then add a glass of wine. Put the lid back on and simmer for about 45 minutes. Remove from the heat and allow the octopus pieces to become cold in their cooking liquid; this helps to make them tender. Drain the octopus and place on a serving dish; sprinkle generously with chopped parsley and serve with sliced, boiled potatoes or, better still, with *papas arrugadas* (see page 110).

RAPE EN SALSA DE ALMENDRAS

Anglerfish in almond sauce ☞ *Catalonia*

1 Peel the almonds and blanch them for about 4-5 minutes in boiling water without salt; drain them then dry them. Dip the slices of fish into the flour, coating both sides and shaking them to eliminate any excess flour. Brown them (one or two at a time if they are big) on both sides in a pan with 6 tablespoons of oil; drain them and put them into an ovenproof dish. Using the oil left in the pan, slowly sauté the almonds, the bread cut into small cubes, and the peeled cloves of garlic, until the latter are pale gold. Pour everything in the pan into a food mixer and grind to a fine paste with a sprig of parsley; transfer the paste to a bowl, stir in the saffron and dilute with half a glass of wine.

2 Sauté the chopped onion in the oil left in the pan (add more fresh oil if necessary); add the almond paste and mix well, stirring gently over low heat for 5-6 minutes. Add one dl (4 fl oz) of fish broth (or even hot water), mix and add salt and pepper to taste. Pour this sauce over the fish slices and bake in the oven, preheated to 180°C (350°F) for 15 minutes. Serve immediately.

Anglerfish (in slices),
  800 g (1 3/4 lb)
1 onion
2 cloves of garlic
1 slice of farmhouse bread
  (without crust)
Peeled almonds (two dozen)
Parsley
Saffron
Plain flour,
  approx. 40 g (4 tbsp)
Fish broth (made from bouillon
  cubes)
Dry white wine
Salt and pepper
Olive oil

Serves:	4
Preparation:	15'
Cooking:	30' ca.
Difficulty:	● ●
Flavour:	● ●
Kcal (per serving):	478
Proteins (per serving):	38
Fats (per serving):	19
Nutritional value:	●

SANCOCHO CANARIO

Sea bass with potatoes ☞ *Canary Islands*

Fillets of sea bass,
  700 g (1 lb 10 oz)
Small potatoes, 600 g (1 1/4 lb)
2 cloves of garlic
1 fresh red pimiento
Caraway seeds
Ground pimiento
Sale
Vinegar

Serves: 4	
Preparation: 20′	
Cooking: 20′	
Difficulty: ● ●	
Flavour: ● ● ●	
Kcal (per serving): 265	
Proteins (per serving): 33	
Fats (per serving): 2	
Nutritional value: ●	

1 For the amount of sea bass fillets required, buy a 1-1.2 Kg (2 1/4 - 2 1/2 lb) of the fish and ask the fishmonger to fillet it for you, then cut these fillets into pieces suitable for cooking. Peel the potatoes (if they are new potatoes, just rinse them well) and cut them into rounds (or leave them whole if they are very small). Put them in a casserole full of slightly salted water, bring to the boil, cover and boil for 10 minutes; add the fish fillets, lower the heat and simmer for another 10 minutes. Drain both the potatoes and the fish, arrange them on a platter and keep in a warm place. Save the cooking liquid.

2 Pound in a mortar (or in a food mixer) the garlic with a pinch of salt, the fresh pimiento, and a pinch each of caraway seeds and ground pimiento; put this paste into a bowl, add 2 tablespoons of vinegar, 2 or 3 pieces of boiled potato (mashed with a fork) and sufficient cooking liquid to obtain a soft but not runny sauce. Serve the fish fillets coated with some of the sauce, putting the rest of it in a sauceboat.

TRUCHAS A LA ZAMORANA

Trout in vinegar ☛ *Castile and León*

Prepare the trout by removing the scales and entrails, then rinse and dry them. Rub a little salt inside and out, then leave the fish in a cool place for about 30 minutes. Pour one and a half litres (2 ½ pt) of cold water into a fish kettle (or a large, deep pan), add 3-4 tablespoons of oil, a couple of tablespoons of vinegar, the peeled and crushed garlic, a sprig of parsley and 4-5 peppercorns. Bring to the boil, add the trout (two at a time if there is not enough room for all four together, and if all guests are to be served at the same time, this will mean using two pans), bring to the boil once more then lower the heat to minimum. Cover the pan and simmer for 7-8 minutes.

Leave the trout to cool for a few minutes in their broth, then serve them with boiled, new potatoes tossed in parsley.

4 single-portion trout
(250 g; 9 oz each, ready for
use), total 1 Kg (2 ¼ lb)
2-3 cloves of garlic
Parsley
Red wine vinegar
Boiled, new potatoes
(for accompaniment)
Salt, peppercorns
Olive oil

Serves: 4
Preparation: 10'+30'
Cooking: 15' ca.
Difficulty: ● ●
Flavour: ● ●
Kcal (per serving): 512
Proteins (per serving): 49
Fats (per serving): 26
Nutritional value: ●

TUMBET DE PESCADO

Fish in cream of vegetable sauce ☛ *Balearic Islands*

Fillets of grouper
  (or other white-meat fish),
  7-800 g (1 3/4 lb)
Potatoes, 500 g (1 lb 2 oz)
2 aubergines
2 sweet peppers
  (red and yellow)
1 onion
1 clove of garlic
2-3 ripe tomatoes
1 lemon
Bay leaf, ground cinnamon
Sugar
Plain flour, 40 g (4 tbsp)
Dry white wine
Frying oil
Olive oil
Coarse salt
Salt and pepper

Serves: 4	
Preparation: 20'+30'	
Cooking: 1h 15'	
Difficulty: ●●●	
Flavour: ●●	
Kcal (per serving): 830	
Proteins (per serving): 43	
Fats (per serving): 37	
Nutritional value: ●●●	

1 Prepare all the vegetables: peel the potatoes and aubergines, slice the latter, put them in a dish and cover them with coarse salt, pressing them down with a weight to let the bitter flavour 'sweat out'. Roast the peppers in the oven until black, then remove the skin and cut them into strips. Put the fish in an ovenproof dish, sprinkle with a little salt and add the juice of the lemon, a few drops of oil and a glass of wine. Bake in the oven, preheated to 200°C (375°F), for 10 minutes. Remove the fish fillets from the dish but save the liquid.

2 Slice the potatoes into rounds and fry them for 2-3 minutes with 4-5 tablespoons of oil in a pan; cover the pan, lower the heat and sauté gently until cooked but still firm, watching that they do not stick to the pan. Rinse the salt from the slices of aubergine, dry them, and then dip them in the flour in a plate until coated on both sides. Pour plenty of frying oil in a pan and fry the aubergines until golden on both sides; remove them from the pan with a draining spoon and leave them to dry on kitchen paper.

A stop in one of the typical, simple meeting places on the shores of Formentera, the smallest of the Balearic Islands.

3 Sauté the finely chopped onion and garlic in a casserole with 5-6 tablespoons of olive oil; add the chopped tomatoes, a bay leaf, half a teaspoon of ground cinnamon, a level teaspoon of sugar, salt and pepper. Pour in the liquid from the fish and simmer for about 10 minutes.

Filter these ingredients then cream them in the mixer; the result should be a fairly thick cream.

4 Oil an ovenproof dish and cover the bottom of it with round slices of potatoes; put the fish fillets over these, then the fried aubergines and the strips of sweet pepper. Repeat these layers until all the vegetables are used up. Top the casserole with the creamed vegetable sauce (see Step 3) and bake in the oven, preheated to 180°C (350°F), for 15 minutes. Serve immediately.

TXANGURRO

Stuffed spider-crab ☞ *Basque Counties*

4 (or 2-3 if bigger) freshly
  caught spider-crabs, approx.
  500 g (1 lb 2 oz) each
1 onion
Tomato purée, 1 dl (4 fl oz)
Parsley
1 fresh red pimiento
Dry breadcrumbs
Dry white wine
Salt and pepper
Butter (optional),
  30 g (1 oz; 2 tbsp)
Olive oil

Serves: 4	
Preparation: 25'	
Cooking: 40' ca.	
Difficulty: ● ● ●	
Flavour: ● ●	
Kcal (per serving): 439	
Proteins (per serving): 36	
Fats (per serving): 19	
Nutritional value: ● ●	

1 Rinse the crabs well then drop them into a pan full of slightly salted, boiling water. Boil for 15 minutes, remove the crabs from the pan and put them in a basin full of cold water to stop them cooking. Place them on their backs on a board, grasp the legs and twist them one by one to detach them; break them open and remove the flesh.

2 Prise the abdomen shell away from the back shell by putting your fingers in the narrow openings between the two, or use the blade of a knife; eliminate the entrails. Extract the dark coloured and white flesh. Save the top shells of the crabs for serving.

3 Peel and finely chop the onion and sauté it slowly in a pan with 4 tablespoons of oil. Add the dark flesh of the crabs, a glass of wine, the tomato purée, the chopped parsley (a sprig), the pimiento, salt and pepper. Simmer for about 15 minutes, adding a little hot water whenever necessary.

4 Add the white flesh, mix a little, then remove from the heat. Distribute this mixture among the shells kept for serving; cover the tops with breadcrumbs and a dab of butter (if preferred) or a few drops of oil. Put the stuffed shells under the grill for 5 minutes and serve immediately. If the flesh in the crabs is not sufficient (it depends on the season when they are caught), use a briefly boiled fillet of sole per person and add these to the mixture.

The splendid San Sebastián Bay, which has one of the most famous beaches in the whole of Spain.

ZARZUELA

Sautéed mixed seafood ☛ *Eastern regions*

1 lobster (or crawfish),
   1 Kg (2 1/4 lb)
Scallops, one dozen
Fresh scampi, one dozen
Mussels, 500 g (1 lb 2 oz)
Large clams, 500 g (1 lb 2 oz)
Lean cured raw ham (one
   piece), 100 g (4 oz)
6-7 ripe tomatoes
3 onions
2 sweet peppers
2 cloves of garlic
1 lemon
Shelled almonds,
   100 g (2 oz; 1/4 cup)
Saffron
Bouquet garni, tied
   (bay leaf, parsley and thyme)
Dry white wine
Salt and pepper
Olive oil

Serves:	6-8
Preparation:	30'
Cooking:	40'
Difficulty:	● ●
Flavour:	● ● ●
Kcal (per serving):	587
Proteins (per serving):	63
Fats (per serving):	23
Nutritional value:	● ●

Clean the mussels (see page 80), the clams and the scallops (extracting the 'nuts' as described on page 20). Scald the lobster in slightly salted boiling water, then open the shell to remove the flesh (eliminate the intestinal tract). Prepare all the vegetables by trimming, rinsing and drying them. Slowly sauté the finely chopped garlic and onions in a large pan (or better still, in the *paellera* pan; see page 54) with 8-10 tablespoons of oil; add the diced sweet peppers and the ham cut into thin strips. Rinse and dry the scampi and toss-fry them in a pan with 2-3 tablespoons of oil for 5 minutes. Add the diced tomatoes, 2 glasses of wine, the juice of the lemon, the bouquet garni and the finely chopped almonds to the large pan (or *paellera*); add salt and pepper to taste, allow the flavours to combine for 5 minutes over high heat, then add a sachet of saffron diluted with a little water, the clams, the mussels, the scallop 'nuts', the lobster flesh (cut into pieces) and the scampi. Stir, lower the heat and cook gently for about ten minutes, until the clams and mussels have opened. Reduce any excess liquid, remove the bouquet garni, sprinkle with chopped parsley and serve.

The meaning of zarzuela? Sometimes this word is mistranslated as 'operetta' but it really means an Iberian type of musical entertainment, much like the French opéra-comique, which first appeared in the 18th century but became popular a century later. The name itself comes from the Zarzuela Palace in Madrid, near the Prado, and more precisely from the zarzas (thorn bushes) which literally covered the spot. The zarzuela show was traditionally a mixture of folk songs and dances, lyrical and narrative airs, rhetorical recitation and musical interludes. A real cocktail of ingredients and colours, just like this dish.

Eggs, OPEN OMELETTES AND VEGETABLES

The abundance
of delicious dishes made with eggs
is proof of how farmhouse
tradition plays a vital role
in Iberian cooking, from the piperrada
to the huevos a la flamenca,
from the revueltos to tortillas,
while the side-dishes made from
vegetables confirm the open-hearted,
happy atmosphere
of the Spanish table.

5

HUEVOS A LA FLAMENCA

Oven-baked eggs with vegetables ☞ *Andalusia*

8 eggs
Cured raw ham (one slice),
    100 g (4 oz)
Chorizo (see page 60),
    100 g (4 oz)
4 ripe tomatoes
Fresh shelled peas,
    100 g (4 oz)
2 artichokes
16 asparagus tips (even
    frozen), optional
1 onion
1 clove of garlic
1 fresh red pimiento
Parsley
Salt and pepper
Olive oil

Serves:	4
Preparation:	20'
Cooking:	40'
Difficulty:	●●
Flavour:	●●●
Kcal (per serving):	637
Proteins (per serving):	35
Fats (per serving):	48
Nutritional value:	●●●

1 Boil the peas in slightly salted water for 7-8 minutes; drain them and keep to one side. Prepare the artichokes by removing the stalks and the tough outer leaves; boil them in slightly salted water for about 10 minutes, then drain them upside down. Peel the onion and chop it finely together with the garlic then sauté them both in a pan with the diced ham and 6 tablespoons of oil. Rinse the tomatoes, remove the seeds, cut into pieces and add to the pan; add salt and pepper to taste then simmer on low heat for about 15 minutes.

2 Distribute this sauce among 4 individual, slightly oiled ovenproof dishes; break two eggs into each one (try to keep the yolks whole), then add the peas, tiny strips of pimiento, the *chorizo* cut into round slices, the artichokes cut into strips and, if desired, the asparagus tips (to cook these, see the next page). Add salt and sprinkle with chopped parsley before putting in the oven, preheated to 180°C (350°F), for 10 minutes. Serve immediately.

HUEVOS A LA VASCA

Eggs with asparagus ☞ *Basque Counties*

1 Rinse the asparagus, tie them into a bunch and stand them upright in a deep pan; add water to just cover the white part of the stalks and boil for 15 minutes. Drain them, eliminate the white stalks and cut the green parts into small pieces. In the meantime, boil the peas in slightly salted water for 7-8 minutes then drain them.

2 Peel the garlic and shallots, chop finely and sauté slowly in a pan with 4-5 tablespoons of oil. Add a tablespoon of flour (taking care to avoid lumps when it mixes with the oil), 1 dl (4 fl oz) of broth, salt and pepper; stir gently until the sauce thickens then distribute it among 4 individual ovenproof dishes, add the pieces of asparagus and the peas, break two eggs into each dish and sprinkle with chopped parsley. Cook *bain-marie* (or in the oven at 160°C; 330°F) for ten minutes, until the yolks are cooked but still soft (when using the oven for cooking, add the parsley just before serving). Serve accompanied by fingers of toasted bread.

8 eggs
12 asparagus (not too big)
Fresh shelled peas,
   100 g (4 oz)
4 cloves of garlic
3 shallots
Parsley
Plain flour
Vegetable broth (made from
   bouillon cubes)
3 slices of toasted farmhouse
   bread (for serving)
Salt and pepper
Olive oil

Serves: 4	
Preparation: 15'	
Cooking: 35'	
Difficulty: ●●	
Flavour: ●●	
Kcal (per serving): 537	
Proteins (per serving): 27	
Fats (per serving): 30	
Nutritional value: ●●	

HUEVOS A LA VIZCAÍNA

Boiled eggs in savoury sauce ☞ *Basque Counties*

8 eggs
1 onion
2 sweet peppers
6 ripe (or 400 g; 1 lb, chopped)
   tomatoes
Fresh shelled peas, 100 g (4 oz)
2-3 cloves of garlic
Parsley
Ground pimiento
Saffron
Plain flour
Salt and pepper
Olive oil

Serves:	4
Preparation:	15'
Cooking:	35'
Difficulty:	● ●
Flavour:	● ● ●
Kcal (per serving):	455
Proteins (per serving):	25
Fats (per serving):	30
Nutritional value:	● ●

1 Boil the eggs for 7 minutes, remove them from the water, cool, then shell them. Boil the peas in water for 4-5 minutes, drain but save the liquid. Peel the onion, rinse the peppers and tomatoes (remove stalks, seeds and fibrous parts). Gently sauté the finely chopped onion and the peppers cut into strips for 7-8 minutes in a pan with 4-5 tablespoons of oil; add a tablespoon of flour very gradually, a pinch of ground pimiento, the diced tomatoes and the peas with 2 ladles of their cooking water. Add salt and pepper to taste.

2 Reduce slowly for about 15 minutes, stirring every now and then. In the meantime, pound the peeled garlic in a mortar, then add a pinch of saffron to the paste obtained. Blend the paste into the sauce, sprinkle with chopped parsley and allow the flavours to combine for a few seconds; gently add the boiled eggs halved lengthwise. Simmer for a further 5-6 minutes, sprinkle some more chopped parsley over the top then serve immediately.

HUEVOS MALLORQUINOS

Eggs with cured meats and vegetables
☞ *Balearic Islands*

1 Clean and trim the carrots and the leek, chop them finely and sauté slowly for 2-3 minutes in a casserole (preferably earthenware) with 2-3 tablespoons of melted lard. Add the peas, stir for a few seconds then cover with broth. Put the lid on the casserole and simmer for about ten minutes. Remove the vegetables from the casserole, drain over the pan so that all the liquid goes back into it, and then purée them in a mixer. Put the purée back in the casserole and reduce slowly over very low heat, stirring all the time until the mixture achieves the consistency of thick cream. Keep this in a warm place.

2 Brown the slices of *sobresata* on both sides in a pan with a few drops of water; keep in a warm place. Prepare the eggs: separate the white from the yolk of one egg and drop the white into the hot pan where the *sobresata* was cooked, adding a knob of lard (do not let the fat become too hot). Cook the egg white on moderate heat, then gently place the yolk in the middle, with a dash of salt and pepper (the yolk must 'veil' over but not cook completely). Repeat these steps for all the other eggs then place each one over a slice of cooked *sobresata* and accompany with the creamed vegetables.

Sobresata *is a large sausage-like delicacy, typical of the Balearic Islands, made of finely minced pork flavoured with a touch of ground pimiento. The* sobrasada *found on the Continent is much hotter in taste. If you cannot find* sobresata, *Milan or Hungarian salami or* cervelas *can be used.*

8 eggs	
Sobresata (see below), 8 slices	
2 carrots	
1 leek	
Fresh shelled peas, 200 g (8 oz)	
Vegetable broth (made from bouillon cubes), approx. half a litre (³/4 pt)	
Salt and pepper	
Lard, 50 g (2 oz; 5 tbsp)	

Serves: 4	
Preparation: 10′	
Cooking: 30′	
Difficulty: ●●	
Flavour: ●●	
Kcal (per serving): 538	
Proteins (per serving): 32	
Fats (per serving): 38	
Nutritional value: ●●●	

REVUELTO DE GAMBAS Y GRELOS

Scrambled eggs with shrimps ☞ *Galicia*

8 eggs
Turnip broccoli, 250 g (9 oz)
Shrimp tails, 100 g (4 oz)
Milk
Salt and white pepper
Olive oil

Serves:	4
Preparation:	10'
Cooking:	10'
Difficulty:	●
Flavour:	● ●
Kcal (per serving):	426
Proteins (per serving):	28
Fats (per serving):	31
Nutritional value:	● ●

1 Whisk the eggs in a bowl with a pinch of salt, a dash of pepper and a few drops of milk. Rinse and prepare the broccoli, boil them for one or two minutes in slightly salted water then drain them well and chop roughly.

2 Sauté the broccoli in a pan over high heat with 3-4 tablespoons of oil, lower the heat and add the shrimp tails; mix and increase the heat to medium then pour the beaten eggs in. Scramble the mixture with an egg whisk and serve immediately.

TORTILLA CAPUCHINA

Potato and asparagus open omelette ☛ *Madrid*

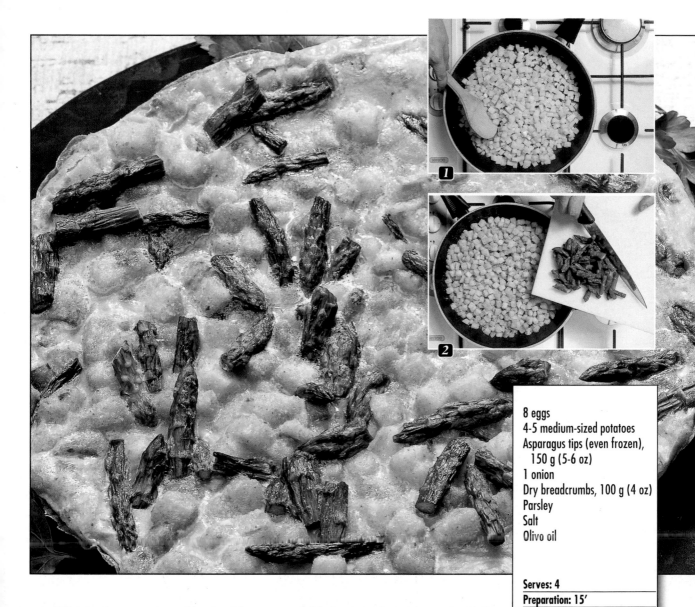

8 eggs
4-5 medium-sized potatoes
Asparagus tips (even frozen),
  150 g (5-6 oz)
1 onion
Dry breadcrumbs, 100 g (4 oz)
Parsley
Salt
Olivo oil

Serves: 4	
Preparation: 15'	
Cooking: 25'	
Difficulty: ● ●	
Flavour: ● ●	
Kcal (per serving): 593	
Proteins (per serving): 29	
Fats (per serving): 30	
Nutritional value: ● ●	

1 Whisk the eggs in a bowl with a pinch of salt and a chopped sprig of parsley; leave to stand. Peel the onion and the potatoes. Chop the onion fine and sauté in a pan with 4-5 tablespoons of oil. Add the potatoes cut into tiny cubes and cook gently for 7-8 minutes, stirring frequently.

2 Add the breadcrumbs and stir for 2 minutes; add the asparagus tips, stir again, then pour in the beaten eggs. Cook the *tortilla* for 3-4 minutes on medium heat, then flip it over and cook the other side.

PIPERRADA VASCA

Sweet pepper open omelette ☛ *Basque Counties*

8 eggs
2 sweet peppers
1 onion
2-3 ripe tomatoes
4 cloves of garlic
Salt
Olive oil

Serves: 4	
Preparation: 15'	
Cooking: 35'	
Difficulty: ● ●	
Flavour: ● ●	
Kcal (per serving): 404	
Proteins (per serving): 23	
Fats (per serving): 29	
Nutritional value: ● ●	

1 Rinse and dry the sweet peppers, eliminating the stalks, seeds and fibrous parts. Bake them in the oven until the skins are black; peel them then cut them into strips.

2 Peel the onion and chop it finely with the peeled garlic and sauté in a pan (preferably earthenware) with 5-6 tablespoons of oil.

3 Add the tomatoes (rinsed, seeds removed, cut into pieces) and the strips of pepper; cook on moderate heat for 15 minutes, mashing the vegetables with a wooden spoon when they become soft and allowing the liquid to reduce, to obtain a sort of purée.

4 Beat the eggs with a pinch of salt and pour into the pan, stirring all the time. Cover the pan and cook over low heat, without turning the omelette over. Serve immediately.

The unmistakable outline of the ultra-modern building that houses Bilbao Museum.

TORTILLA MURCIANA

Sweet pepper and aubergine open omelette
☞ *Murcia and Eastern regions*

6 eggs
3 ripe tomatoes
4 sweet peppers
1 aubergine
Salt
Olive oil

Serves:	4
Preparation:	15'+30'
Cooking:	25'
Difficulty:	● ●
Flavour:	● ● ●
Kcal (per serving):	410
Proteins (per serving):	23
Fats (per serving):	29
Nutritional value:	● ●

Rinse the aubergine but do not peel it; cut it into slices and sprinkle coarse salt over them on a plate, pressing them down with a weight for 30 minutes to sweat out the bitter taste. Rinse and dry the slices then cut them into small cubes. Rinse the sweet peppers, remove their stalks, seeds and fibrous parts and cut into strips.
Rinse the tomatoes, remove the seeds, cut into tiny pieces and sauté in a pan with 3-4 tablespoons of oil; add the sweet pepper strips and the aubergine cubes and simmer gently for about ten minutes, stirring frequently. Whisk the eggs in a bowl with a pinch of salt and pour into the pan. Cook the *tortilla* over medium heat, then flip it over and cook the other side. Serve cut into wedges.

BERENJENAS A LA CATALANA

Aubergines with walnuts ☛ *Catalonia*

3 aubergines
Kernels of 6-7 walnuts
1 onion
2 cloves of garlic
2 tomatoes
Parsley
A small amount of vegetable broth (made from bouillon cubes)
Salt and pepper
Olive oil

Serves: 4	
Preparation: 15'+30'	
Cooking: 30'	
Difficulty: ●●	
Flavour: ●●	
Kcal (per serving): 256	
Proteins (per serving): 7	
Fats (per serving): 20	
Nutritional value: ●●	

1 Peel the aubergines and cut them into slices; put these on a plate, sprinkle them with salt then weigh them down for about 30 minutes to 'sweat out' the bitter taste. Stir-fry the walnut kernels in a casserole with 5 tablespoons of oil; remove them with a draining spoon and dry them on kitchen paper. Rinse and dry the aubergines, cut them into cubes and fry them for 2-3 minutes over high heat in the oil left in the pan; add the chopped onion and garlic, stir and cook for a further 2-3 minutes.

2 Lower the heat, add the rinsed tomatoes (without seeds and cut into pieces). Pound the walnut kernels in a mortar then dilute the paste obtained with half a glass of warm vegetable broth; pour this sauce into the casserole and add salt and pepper to taste. Continue cooking over low heat until the aubergines are soft. Serve sprinkled with chopped parsley.

BERENJENAS RELLENAS

Aubergines with meat stuffing ☞ *Balearic Islands*

4 aubergines
Minced, lean pork (or chicken),
  200 g (8 oz)
Cured raw ham, 50 g (2 oz)
1 onion
1 tomato
2 eggs
Ground cinnamon and nutmeg
Plain flour and dry
  breadcrumbs
Milk, 1 dl (4 fl oz)
Dry white wine
Salt and pepper
Olive oil

Serves: 4-6	
Preparation: 15'+30'	
Cooking: 30'	
Difficulty: ●●	
Flavour: ●●	
Kcal (per serving): 493	
Proteins (per serving): 22	
Fats (per serving): 25	
Nutritional value: ●●●	

The XVIII San Rafael Church, in the middle of Ibiza countryside.

1 Rinse the aubergines and cut them into two lengthwise; remove the pulp with a teaspoon, taking care to not perforate the 'hulls' of the 8 little boats that will be left. Oil them lightly both inside and out and place them on an oven tray; cook in the oven, preheated to 160°C (330°F), for about 30 minutes. In the meantime, purée the pulp in a food mixer and keep to one side.

2 Brown the meat with the finely chopped ham in a pan with 3-4 tablespoons of oil; when the meat has browned, add the peeled and chopped onion, the aubergine purée and cook over medium heat for 4-5 minutes, stirring frequently. Add the rinsed tomato, without seeds and cut into pieces, a pinch of ground cinnamon and half a glass of wine; allow the wine to evaporate and reduce the sauce, stirring all the time.

3 Heat (but do not allow to 'smoke') a couple of tablespoons of oil in a small casserole then gradually blend in a heaped tablespoon of flour (stirring all the time to avoid the formation of lumps) and the milk; continue stirring over low heat for 3-4 minutes until the white sauce thickens, adding salt and pepper to taste and a little grated nutmeg. Blend the white sauce into the meat mixture in a bowl and add a beaten egg.

4 Line an oven dish with grease-proof paper and arrange the aubergine 'boats' in it; stuff the aubergines with the mixture, level the surfaces and brush them with beaten egg; sprinkle breadcrumbs over the tops and add a few drops of oil to each one. Bake in the oven, preheated to 180°C (350), for 15 minutes then serve.

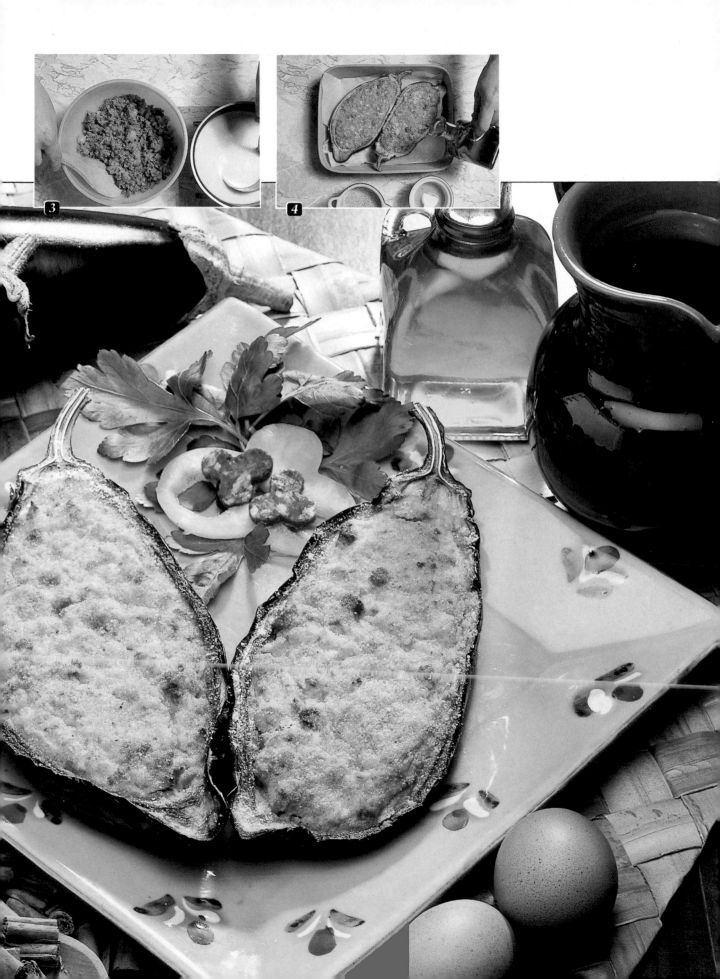

COLIFLOR AL AJO ARRIERO

Cauliflower with garlic and vinegar ☞ *Aragona*

Rinse the cauliflower and divide it into florets, eliminating the core. Bring a pot full of slightly salted water to the boil then cook the cauliflower in it (without a lid) for 12 minutes; drain and arrange the florets on a serving dish. Keep the water where they were cooked.

Peel and finely chop the garlic and sauté it in a pan with 7-8 tablespoons of oil; as soon as it starts to become golden, take the pan off the heat and add a teaspoonful of ground pimiento, a tablespoon of vinegar, the chopped parsley and sufficient cooking liquid to obtain a not too thin sauce. Pour this sauce over the cauliflower florets. This dish makes an excellent accompaniment to meat, and even filleted fish.

The majestic outline of the Basilica de Nuestra Señora del Pilar, in Saragozza.

1 medium-sized cauliflower
4-5 cloves of garlic
Ground pimiento
Parsley
Red wine vinegar
Salt
Olive oil

Serves: 4	
Preparation: 15′	
Cooking: 20′	
Difficulty: ●	
Flavour: ● ● ●	
Kcal (per serving): 150	
Proteins (per serving): 4	
Fats (per serving): 10	
Nutritional value: ●	

FAVES AL TOMBET

Beans with lettuce ☛ *Eastern regions*

If dry beans are being used, soak them for 3-4 hours before starting to prepare this dish. Rinse and trim the lettuce, eliminate the core, and roughly chop it up.

Fry the slice of bread in a casserole (preferably earthenware) with the peeled garlic and 5-6 tablespoons of oil; drain both the bread and the garlic, pound them in a mortar (or food mixer) to obtain a paste, adding half a teaspoon of ground pimiento and a tablespoon of vinegar.

Drain the beans and slowly sauté them for about 15 minutes in the oil left in the casserole, together with the chopped lettuce; add the paste containing the bread, 2-3 ladles of broth, a pinch of salt and pepper. Cover the casserole and simmer for about 30 minutes. Serve immediately. This is excellent served with eggs or *tortillas*.

Fresh, white haricot beans (podded), 700 g or 350 g if dry beans are used (1 lb 10 oz or 14 oz)
1 head of lettuce
2-3 cloves of garlic
1 slice of farmhouse bread (without crust)
Ground pimiento
Red wine vinegar
Vegetable broth (made with bouillon cubes)
Salt and pepper
Olive oil

Serves:	4
Preparation:	15'+4h
Cooking:	50'
Difficulty:	●●
Flavour:	●●●
Kcal (per serving):	451
Proteins (per serving):	24
Fats (per serving):	12
Nutritional value:	●●

FABADA ASTURIANA

Beans with cured meats and pig's trotters ☞ *Asturias*

1 Soak the beans for about two hours in cold water. At the same time, cover the *lacón* with warm water and leave it there until needed. If the smoked sausages (*morcilla*) are heavily encrusted, scrape any excess off the skins. Boil the bacon in unsalted water for 4-5 minutes. Drain the beans, put them in a large earthenware casserole and cover them with water so that there is two centimetres (just over an inch) of water above the beans; bring to the boil over high heat, removing the scum which forms on the surface of the liquid. Add a pinch of saffron diluted with a drop of warm water.

2 Add the *lacón* and the bacon, stirring them into the beans so that they are covered. Put the lid on the casserole and cook for 5-6 minutes; remove the scum once more from the broth.

3 Add the *chorizo* and *morcilla*, both sliced, cover the pot again and cook for another 5-6 minutes, removing the scum as before. Then add 2 bay leaves, lower the heat to minimum and simmer very, very slowly for at least two and a half hours.

4 Check that the beans remain covered with liquid; if the broth should dry out, add a little water (always hot water). To avoid the food sticking to the casserole, shake it every now and then, but do not stir the ingredients. If the *fabada* appears to contain too much liquid, take the lid off the casserole for the last 10-15 minutes of cooking time. When the cooking time is up, the beans should be soft but not disintegrated or split. Remove from the heat and allow the food to cool in the casserole for 15 minutes before serving.

Morcilla, *which must not be confused with* butifarra negra (see page 22) *is a blood sausage about the same diameter as a normal sausage, with tiny bits of fat here and there in the mixture and, depending on the region where it is made, flavoured with aniseed, cinnamon, cloves and pine nuts. In the Asturias region it is generally smoked, as is the* chorizo (see page 60). *Lacón (called paleta in other regions) is salt-cured pig's trotter; if you cannot find it, you may use fresh pig's trotter, and in this case, there will be no need to soak it. Instead of the* morcilla, *you can use blood sausage or smoked salami.*

Dry white haricot beans,
  500 g (1 lb 2 oz)
Smoked *morcilla* (see opposite
  page), 250 g (9 oz)
Smoked *chorizo* (see opposite
  page), 250 g (9 oz)
Unsmoked bacon, 100 g (4 oz)

Lacón (see opposite page), 250 g
  (9 oz)
Saffron
Bay leaf

Serves: 6	
Preparation: 20'+2h 15'	
Cooking: 3h ca.	
Difficulty: ● ●	
Flavour: ● ● ●	
Kcal (per serving): 738	
Proteins (per serving): 35	
Fats (per serving): 46	
Nutritional value: ● ● ●	

3

4

HABAS A LA RONDEÑA

Beans with cured raw ham ☞ *Andalusia*

Fresh, white haricot beans,
  700 g or 350 g if dry beans
  are used (1 lb 10 oz or 14 oz)
Cured raw ham (one slice),
  100 g (4 oz)
2 eggs
2 spring onions
1 ripe tomato
1 clove of garlic
Salt and pepper
Olive oil

Serves:	4-6
Preparation:	15'+4-5h
Cooking:	45'
Difficulty:	●●
Flavour:	●●
Kcal (per serving):	501
Proteins (per serving):	24
Fats (per serving):	28
Nutritional value:	●●●

If dry beans are being used, remember to soak them in cold water for 4-5 hours before starting to prepare this dish. Boil the eggs for 7 minutes until hard. Peel the onions and chop them with the garlic, then sauté them in a casserole (preferable earthenware) with 3-4 tablespoons of oil. Rinse the tomato, remove the seeds, and cut it into pieces; add these to the casserole together with the diced ham, the beans, and a pinch of salt and pepper. Pour in hot water until it almost covers the beans, put the lid on the casserole, bring to the boil, lower the heat and simmer for at least half an hour. Remove the casserole from the heat when the beans are cooked but not too soft (*al dente*) and stir the contents. Serve immediately with slices of boiled egg as garnish.

JUDÍAS VERDES A LA CASTELLANA

String beans with sweet peppers ☛ *Castile and La Mancha*

| String beans, 500 g (1 lb 2 oz) |
| 3 sweet peppers |
| (different colours) |
| 3 cloves of garlic |
| Parsley |
| Salt and freshly ground pepper |
| Olive oil |

Serves:	4
Preparation:	20′
Cooking:	30′
Difficulty:	●
Flavour:	● ● ●
Kcal (per serving):	121
Proteins (per serving):	3
Fats (per serving):	10
Nutritional value:	●

Top and tail the beans and remove the filament; rinse and drain them. Boil the prepared beans in plenty of slightly salted water (bring to the boil before adding the beans) for about 20 minutes, then drain them in a sieve. In the meantime, roast the sweet peppers under the grill of the oven, turning them over every now and then; remove the skins, stalks, seeds and fibrous parts and cut them into strips.

Sauté the peeled, chopped garlic in a pan with 4-5 tablespoons of oil; add the beans and sweet pepper and quickly stir-fry, adding salt and freshly ground pepper to taste. Serve sprinkled with chopped parsley.

PAPAS ARRUGADAS

New potatoes cooked in salt ☞ *Canary Islands*

New potatoes,
 600 g (1 1/4 lb)
Coarse salt

Serves: 4	
Preparation: 5′	
Cooking: 30′	
Difficulty: ●	
Flavour: ●●●	
Kcal (per serving): 130	
Proteins (per serving): 4	
Fats (per serving): 0	
Nutritional value: ●	

*P*apas arrugadas are tiny, new potatoes boiled in sea water; if no sea water is available then household tap water can be used, adding a tablespoon of coarse salt for every litre (1 2/3 pt) of water. Boil the potatoes in their skins until they are cooked but firm (*al dente*), drain them well and place them in an ovenproof dish and bakc in the oven, preheated to 220°C (410°F), for 12 minutes. Serve immediately (remember that they are already salted) as an accompaniment to Canary Island dishes, or other dishes of roast fish or meat.

PATATAS A LA RIOJANA

Garlic potatoes with eggs ☞ *La Rioja*

1 Pound the peeled garlic, about ten peppercorns and the dry pimiento (without seeds) in a mortar; add a teaspoon of ground pimiento and a pinch of salt, and keep to one side. Peel the potatoes, cut them in half, then into slices 5-6 mm ($^2/_3$ inch) thick. Fry them very slowly in a pan (with a lid) in 4-5 tablespoons of oil, turning them over with a spatula so that both sides brown.

2 Add the garlic paste diluted with a ladle of warm water; cover the pan and simmer for about 20 minutes. In the meantime, boil the eggs (7 minutes) until hard then shell them. Serve the potatoes garnished with slices of boiled egg, preferably as an accompaniment to pork dishes (but they are excellent served with *tortillas* and grilled fish or crustaceans).

6-7 medium-sized potatoes, approx. 600 g (1 $^1/_4$ lb)	
2 eggs	
2-3 cloves of garlic	
1 dry red pimiento	
Ground pimiento	
Salt and peppercorns	
Olive oil	

Serves: 4	
Preparation: 20'	
Cooking: 20' ca.	
Difficulty: ●●	
Flavour: ●●●	
Kcal (per serving): 351	
Proteins (per serving): 11	
Fats (per serving): 15	
Nutritional value: ●●●	

PURRUSALDA

Leeks with potatoes ☞ *Basque Counties*

Leeks, 750 g (1 lb 12 oz)
Small potatoes, 500 g (1 lb 2 oz)
2 cloves of garlic
Ground pimiento
Bay leaf
Vegetable broth
  (made with bouillon cubes),
  2.5 dl (10 fl oz)
Salt and pepper
Olive oil

Serves:	6
Preparation:	20'
Cooking:	45'
Difficulty:	● ●
Flavour:	● ● ●
Kcal (per serving):	193
Proteins (per serving):	4
Fats (per serving):	11
Nutritional value:	●

1 Clean and trim the leeks, cutting them into rings up to where the white of the stalks becomes green. Sauté the garlic in a pan (preferably earthenware) with 4-5 tablespoons of oil; remove the garlic from the pan as soon as it becomes golden (but do not discard it) and then, in its place, sauté the leeks very, very slowly.

2 Peel the potatoes and cut them into round slices as near as possible the same thickness as the leeks; add them to the leeks in the pan, together with a bay leaf and a pinch of salt and pepper. Pour in the broth, then add the fried garlic after pounding it in a mortar with a teaspoon of ground pimiento. Stir to blend, cover and simmer for about 30 minutes. Serve as an accompaniment to fish dishes.

CAKES AND DESSERTS

*This is where Iberian imagination
is really let loose, and where we find
the Spanish love of household traditions,
fine food and secrets 'borrowed'
from convents.
Country-style torrijas made from bread
and artistically produced pastries.
Basque walnuts, Andalusian almonds,
Canary Island sweet potatoes
and bananas:
delicacies to tempt you over
and over again!*

6

BRAZO DE GITANO

Swiss-roll with custard ☞ *Andalusia*

1 To make the *cremadina* (custard) for the filling, slowly heat the milk (do not allow to boil) in a pot with the piece of cinnamon and the vanilla pod. In the meantime, beat the egg yolks, sugar, flour and salt together with a hand mixer until the mixture is soft and smooth.

2 Put this mixture into a bowl suitable for cooking over warm water (*bain-marie*). Bring the water in the pan under the bowl to a moderate boil, then add the hot milk after removing the cinnamon and vanilla pod. Stirring gently, heat the mixture until it just reaches boiling point; add two tablespoons of hot water and lower the heat to minimum. Cook for 10 minutes, stirring gently all the time.

3 Remove the bowl from the water and add the butter cut into small pieces. Mix well and allow the *cremadina* to cool; this will thicken and will be used for filling the *brazo de gitano*.

4 To make the *brazo* (sponge-cake), whip the whites of the eggs until stiff in a bowl; add the egg yolks one at a time, then the sugar, the flour and the grated rind of the lemon. Use butter to grease a rectangular cake tin (about 30 cm x 35 cm; 12 x 14 inches) and line it with greaseproof paper (buttered on the surface which will come into contact with the cake). Pour the sponge mixture into the tin, smoothing the surface; bake in an oven previously heated to 180°C (350°F) for approximately 15 min.

5 Remove the cake tin from the oven, dust a sufficiently large sheet of greaseproof paper with icing sugar and carefully turn the sponge out onto this. Spread the *cremadina* in a thick layer over the sponge, leaving a little custard for decoration.

6 Using the greaseproof paper under the sponge, gently roll up the *brazo* and put it on a cake plate with the free end of the sponge underneath and out of sight. Spread the remaining *cremadina* over the roll and dust with icing sugar.

For the cremadina:	For the sponge-cake:	Serves: 6
2 egg-yolks	6 eggs	Preparation: 35'
Castor sugar, 20 g (2 tbsp)	Castor sugar, 80 g (6 tbsp)	Cooking: 45' ca.
Plain flour, 15 g (1 $^1/_2$ tbsp)	Plain flour, 80 g (7-8 tbsp)	Difficulty: ● ● ●
Full milk, approx. 2 dl (8 fl oz)	1 lemon	Kcal (per serving): 294
Small piece of cinnamon	Icing sugar	Proteins (per serving): 6
1 vanilla pod (or a drop of extract)	Butter, 40 g (2 oz; 3 tbsp)	Fats (per serving): 14
Pinch of salt		Nutritional value: ● ● ●
Butter, 30 g (1 $^1/_2$ oz; 3 tbsp)		

BUÑUELOS DE BONIATOS

Sweet potato fritters ☛ *Canary Islands*

4 *boniatos* (sweet potatoes)
Castor sugar, 30 g (2-3 tbsp)
Sweet wine (*passito* type)
Dry white wine
1 lemon
Plain flour, 30 g (3 tbsp) plus
   extra for the flouring the
   pastry-board
Full milk
Salt
Frying oil

Serves:	4-6
Preparation:	25'
Cooking:	35'
Difficulty:	●●
Kcal (per serving):	533
Proteins (per serving):	6
Fats (per serving):	27
Nutritional value:	●●●

1 Boil the sweet potatoes in slightly salted water for 15 minutes; drain, remove the skins and mash the potatoes. Put the mashed pulp into a bowl, stir in a glass of sweet wine and half a glass of dry wine, the juice of the lemon, the flour and the sugar. Mix well. If the mixture appears too stiff, soften it with a drop of cold milk.

2 Take a level tablespoon of the mixture and roll it between the palms of the hands to form a ball, giving it the shape of a date; put this on a lightly floured pastry-board or on a clean kitchen towel. Repeat these steps until all the mixture has been used up. Deep-fry only a few of the *buñuelos* at a time in very hot oil, removing them and draining them as soon as they become golden. Serve hot (though they are also excellent cold).

CASADIELLES

Walnut pastries ☞ *Galicia and Asturias*

FLAKY PASTRY:
Mix 175 g (7 oz; 1 1/2 cups) of flour with enough water to make a ball of smooth, springy dough, which will then be set aside wrapped in a kitchen towel. Mix the remaining flour with the softened butter, working it into a rectangular pat; allow to stand for 30 minutes. On a floured pastry-board, roll out the first dough (ball) to about 8 mm (3/4 inch) thick, place the second dough (pat) in the centre and fold the pastry over it. Roll out once more, then fold again into a rectangular pat; put in the fridge for 15 minutes. Remove the dough from the fridge, roll it out, fold as before, and then put it back into the fridge. Repeat these steps three times then roll out the pastry to the desired thickness. Frozen flaky pastry may be used instead.

Finely grind the walnut kernels together with the sugar in a mixer. Dilute a small glass of liqueur with a glass of water and pour into a pan; add a piece of cinnamon and the lemon rind (taking care to remove the white pith). Bring to the boil and boil the syrup slowly for 5 minutes. Remove the cinnamon and lemon rind and add the walnut mixture; stirring continuously, cook for 2-3 minutes, remove from the heat and allow to cool. Roll out the pastry (see method top right), cut it into 10 cm (6 1/2 inch) squares; put a little walnut mixture in the centre of the squares, leaving the borders free. Fold the squares in three, moistening the overlapping edges of the pastry and pressing gently (without squashing) to seal. Press down the sides of the 'parcels' with the prongs (back) of a fork, to seal and garnish. Place the *casadielles*, sealed part downwards, on a baking tin lined with buttered, greaseproof paper; brush all over with beaten egg and bake until golden-brown (12-15 minutes) in the oven preheated to 220°C (410°F).

24 walnut kernels, approx. 200 g (8 oz)
Castor sugar, 100 g (4 oz)
2 egg yolks
Aniseed liqueur
Cinnamon
1 piece of lemon rind
Butter, 30 g (1 oz; 2 tbsp)

For the flaky pastry:
Plain flour, 250 g (9 oz; 2 cups) plus extra for flouring the pastry-board
Butter, 250 g (9 oz)

Serves: 6	
Preparation: 30'+1h 15'	
Cooking: 25'	
Difficulty: ● ● ●	
Kcal (per serving): 874	
Proteins (per serving): 17	
Fats (per serving): 59	
Nutritional value: ● ● ●	

CREMA CATALANA

Oven-baked custard ☞ *Catalonia*

8 egg yolks
Castor sugar, 150 g (6 oz)
Demerara sugar, 50 g (2 oz)
Full milk, 1 litre (1 2/3 pt)
Plain flour,
   20 g (1/2 oz; 1 3/4 tbsp)
Piece of lemon rind
Piece of cinnamon

Serves:	6
Preparation:	20'+2h
Cooking:	30'
Difficulty:	● ●
Kcal (per serving):	404
Proteins (per serving):	19
Fats (per serving):	17
Nutritional value:	● ● ●

Pour the milk (all except half a glass) into a pan with the lemon rind (without the white pith) and the small piece of cinnamon; bring to the boil then remove immediately from the heat. Cover the pan with a lid and leave to one side for about ten minutes. In the meantime, put the egg yolks into a bowl and beat them to a cream with a hand mixer. Remove the lemon rind and cinnamon stick from the milk, then stir it into the creamed eggs, together with the flour mixed with the remaining half glass of milk. Put the contents of the bowl into a pan and beat continuously over low heat until the custard starts to thicken. Remove from the heat as soon as it starts to boil and pour the custard into individual ovenproof ramekins. Wait until the custard becomes cold then put the ramekins into the fridge for about two hours. A few minutes before the dessert is to be served, switch on the grill of the oven; sprinkle a little demerara sugar over the custard in each ramekin then briefly brown the surface under the grill, making the sugar become toffee. This last step must be performed as quickly as possibly so that the custard inside remains cold.

ENSAIMADAS MALLORQUINAS

Sweet twists ☛ *Balearic Islands*

1 Dissolve the yeast in 2-3 tablespoons of lukewarm water and blend it into 100 g (4 oz) of flour and a tablespoon of sugar in a bowl. Cover the bowl with a damp kitchen towel and leave to rise in a warm place for one hour. When the dough has risen, blend the remaining flour and sugar in another bowl, together with the pinch of salt and the eggs; knead the mixture with sufficient water to obtain a smooth dough, then incorporate the risen dough. Turn out onto a floured pastry-board and knead at length, gradually adding 2 tablespoons of olive oil, until the dough is smooth and springy. Grease a large bowl, put the dough in it, cover with a kitchen towel and leave to rise again for 2 hours; this time it will double its size. Knead the risen dough for a few minutes, and then divide it into balls weighing about 40 g (1 1/2 oz) each.

2 Roll out one of these balls as thin as possible, and brush the surface with softened lard. Make it into a ball again then, under the palms of both hands, roll it back and forth until it becomes about 25 cm (10 inches) long and the thickness of a pencil. Twist this into a tight spiral, press the ends to seal them, then place the twist on a baking tray lined with lightly greased oven paper. Repeat these steps until all the dough has been used up, arranging the twists side by side on the tray but not too near each other. Cover the tray with the same towel as before and leave for about 30 minutes. After this, remove the towel, sprinkle some water over the twists and put the tray in the oven, preheated to 200°C (375°F) to bake for a good ten minutes. Remove the *ensaimadas* from the oven and sift icing sugar over them.

Plain flour, 500 g (1 lb 2 oz) plus extra for flouring the pastry-board
2 eggs
Baker's yeast, 10 g (1/2 oz)
Castor sugar, 80 g (3 oz; 1/2 cup)
Icing sugar
Pinch of salt
Lard, 50 g (2 oz)
Olive oil

Serves: 4	
Preparation: 40'+3h 30'	
Cooking: 20' ca.	
Difficulty: ● ● ●	
Kcal (per serving): 752	
Proteins (per serving): 16	
Fats (per serving): 29	
Nutritional value: ● ● ●	

FILLOAS DULCES

Cheese crêpes ☞ *Galicia*

Queso fresco or *requesón* (soft,
    fresh cheese), 200 g (8 oz)
Fresh cream, 2 dl (8 fl oz)
Castor sugar, 50 g (2 oz)
1 lemon
Vanilla extract
Ground cinnamon
Assorted fresh berries
    (optional), 150 g (6 oz)
Lard, 30 g (1 oz)

For the batter:
3 eggs
Full milk, 1 dl (4 fl oz)
Plain flour, 30 g (1 oz)
Pinch of salt
Butter, 20 g (^{3}/4 oz; 1 ^{1}/2 tbsp)

Serves: 4-6	
Preparation: 20'	
Cooking: 20'	
Difficulty: ● ● ●	
Kcal (per serving): 711	
Proteins (per serving): 23	
Fats (per serving): 52	
Nutritional value: ● ● ●	

1 Break the eggs into a basin, or into the bowl of the mixer, and beat them while adding the milk, flour and a pinch of salt; add the melted butter and sufficient water to obtain a thick batter.

2 Grease a 24 cm (10 inch) diameter pan (preferably made of cast-iron) with lard and heat it slowly until it becomes very hot, but do not allow the lard to 'smoke'. Pour enough batter into the pan to cover the bottom of it, allow it to cook on one side (bubbles will appear in the mixture) then toss it like a pancake to turn it over (or use a plate), to cook the other side. If the pan has reached the right temperature, the crêpe should not stick and it will be easy to turn it over. Repeat these steps until all the batter has been used up, greasing the pan with lard again whenever necessary; put the crêpes into a pile one on top of the other on a platter and keep in a warm place.

3 Put the soft cheese in a large bowl, whip it up with a hand mixer, adding the cream, sugar, grated lemon rind and a drop of vanilla essence.

4 Spread this mixture over each crêpe, leaving a border of 2 cm (1 ^{1}/4 inch) all around (if wished, fresh berries may be added); roll up the crêpes and sprinkle ground cinnamon over them. In Galicia, these sometimes have savoury fillings, such as cheese and shellfish.

Young dancers dressed in the local costume perform one of the Galician folk dances.

FLAÕ

Cheese flan ☞ *Balearic Islands*

4 eggs
Queso fresco or *requesón* (soft, fresh cheese), 400 g (12 oz)
Castor sugar, 150 g (6 oz)
Honey
Fresh mint
Aniseed liqueur
Icing sugar
Butter, 30 g (1 oz; 2 tbsp)

For the pastry:
Plain flour, 180 g (8 oz; 1 ¹/₂ cups), plus extra for flouring the pastry-board
1 egg
Full milk
Aniseed liqueur
Pinch of salt
Butter, 50 g (2 oz; 3 ¹/₂ tbsp)

Serves:	4-6
Preparation:	35'+30'
Cooking:	45'
Difficulty:	● ● ●
Kcal (per serving):	1201
Proteins (per serving):	48
Fats (per serving):	59
Nutritional value:	● ● ●

1 To prepare the pastry, put the flour into a large bowl with a pinch of salt, the softened butter (in tiny pieces), a teaspoon of liqueur and the egg. Blend with the beaters of the hand-mixer, adding sufficient warm milk to obtain a smooth but stiff dough, which will then be put in a cool place for 30 minutes. In the meantime, heat the oven to 180°C (350°F). Break the other four eggs into another bowl and, using a hand-mixer, beat them together with the soft cheese, the sugar, 3 tablespoons of honey, the washed and chopped leaves from a sprig of mint, and a tablespoon of liqueur. Beat slowly and at length until all the sugar has dissolved.

2 Roll out the pastry on a floured pastry-board. Grease a 24 cm (10 inch) diameter fluted flan tin with butter and line it with the pastry. Pour the filling into the pastry case, smooth the surface with a spatula, then bake in the oven for about 45 minutes. Remove from the tin, sprinkle with icing sugar and decorate with little sprigs of mint. This cheese cake is best eaten cold.

LINTXAURSALSA

Walnut cream ☞ *Basque Counties*

| 24 walnut kernels, approx. 200 g (8 oz) |
| 4 slices of farmhouse bread, without crusts and toasted |
| Castor sugar, 300 g (10 oz; 2 1/2 cups) |
| Full milk, 2 litres (3 1/4 pt) |

Serves:	4
Preparation:	20'+4h
Cooking:	45'
Difficulty:	● ●
Kcal (per serving):	650
Proteins (per serving):	14
Fats (per serving):	25
Nutritional value:	● ● ●

Finely chop 150 g (6 oz) of walnuts, preferably by hand. Finely grind the toasted bread (without crusts) in a mixer. Pour the milk into a pan, add the sugar, ground bread and chopped walnuts; bring to the boil, lower the heat to minimum and simmer for 45 minutes, stirring continuously to blend all the ingredients well. The cream must become thick and smooth. Remove from the heat, allow to cool, then divide it into serving glasses, decorate the surfaces with the remaining walnuts and store in the fridge for 4 hours. This delicacy is traditionally eaten on Christmas Eve.

LECHE FRITA

Fried milk triangles ☛ *Galicia*

Plain flour,
 220 g (10 oz; 1 ¹/₂ cups)
Castor sugar,
 170 g (7 oz; 1 ¹/₄ cups)
Fine, dry breadcrumbs,
 60 g (6-8 tbsp)
Full milk, half a litre
 (³/₄ pt; 2 cups)
Small piece of cinnamon
Rind of one lemon, in strips
Orange marmalade (or cherry
 jam), as accompaniment
Butter, 140 g (5 oz; ³/₄ cup)
Frying oil

Serves:	4-6
Preparation:	20'+4h
Cooking:	40'
Difficulty:	● ●
Kcal (per serving):	1101
Proteins (per serving):	20
Fats (per serving):	72
Nutritional value:	● ● ●

1 Pour the milk into a small pot and add the cinnamon and the lemon rind (eliminate the white pith); heat slowly and remove from heat as soon as it starts to boil. Slowly melt the butter in a casserole and gradually add 180 g (7 oz) of flour, then 150 g (6 oz) of sugar. Add the milk (after removing the cinnamon and lemon rind) and whip up with a beater (or a hand mixer).

2 The mixture must be soft and creamy; when it starts to boil, remove the casserole from the heat and add the egg yolks, one at a time (keep the whites of the eggs).

3 Put the creamy mixture into a dish lined with grease-proof paper (the dish must be shallow but deep enough for the mixture to be about 2 cm (1 ¹/₄ inches) deep), level the surface and allow it to set in the fridge for 3-4 hours. When set, turn the cream out onto a pastry board and cut it into even triangles, 4-5 cm (3-3 ¹/₂ inches) per side.

4 Coat the triangles with the remaining flour, shaking off any excess flour; dip them into the beaten egg whites (not whipped), then in the breadcrumbs. Deep fry in very hot oil, turning them over when the first side is golden crisp. Drain, dredge with sugar and serve (they are also excellent eaten cold). The fried triangles are occasionally eaten with orange marmalade or cherry jam.

The Cathedral in Santiago de Compostela, since hundreds of years ago the destination of pilgrims from every part of Europe and from all over the world.

TORRIJAS

Fried bread with honey ☞ *Castile La Mancha*

Slightly stale farmhouse bread,
   8 slices (without crusts)
2 eggs
Honey
Dry white wine
Castor sugar and ground
   cinnamon (for serving)
Frying oil

Serves: 4	
Preparation: 20′	
Cooking: 15′	
Difficulty: ● ●	
Kcal (per serving): 644	
Proteins (per serving): 12	
Fats (per serving): 30	
Nutritional value: ● ● ●	

With the aid of pastry-cutters, cut the slices of bread into rounds (4-5 cm; 3-3 $1/2$ inches diameter) and squares (4-5 cm; 3-3 $1/2$ inches per side); put these on a large plate and sprinkle them with the wine mixed with a teaspoon of honey diluted in warm water. After two minutes, turn them over; after a further two minutes, remove them from the plate, drain them (without squeezing them) then put them into the beaten eggs, where they must stay for a few minutes. Fry until golden crisp on both sides in abundant hot oil; remove and drain on kitchen paper. Serve dusted with castor sugar and ground cinnamon.

TORTITAS DE PLÁTANOS

Banana fritters ☞ *Canary Islands*

Peel the bananas and purée them in a mixer (or squash them with the prongs of a fork) then put the purée into a bowl. Beating with a hand mixer, add the eggs, milk, salt, half a teaspoon of cinnamon and the grated lemon rind. When everything has been mixed, add the raising powder, the flour and a liqueur-glass of rum. Leave the batter to stand for 30 minutes, then drop tablespoonfuls of the mixture into abundant hot oil. Remove the fritters with a draining spoon when they are golden crisp and dry them on kitchen paper. Pour a little honey over them before serving (if the honey is too thick, dilute it with a little warm water).

4 bananas
3 eggs
Plain flour,
   100 g (4 oz; ³/4 cup)
Full milk, 1 dl (4 fl oz)
Raising powder, 10 g (¹/2 oz)
Ground cinnamon
Grated rind of half a lemon
Rum
Pinch of salt
Honey (for garnish)
Frying oil

Serves: 4
Preparation: 20'+30'
Cooking: 20'
Difficulty: ● ●
Kcal (per serving): 799
Proteins (per serving): 11
Fats (per serving): 31
Nutritional value: ● ● ●